BRITISH IMPERIALISM

BRITISH IMPERIALISM

Gold, God, Glory

Edited by ROBIN W. WINKS

Yale University

HOLT, RINEHART AND WINSTON

New York • Chicago • San Francisco • Toronto • London

To my mother

Cover illustration: A British infantry soldier with a new magazine rifle. *(The Bettmann Archive)*

Library of Congress Catalog Card Number: 63—14412
03-012260-0

Printed in the United States of America
90123 45 98

Cover engraving courtesy of Bettman Archives

CONTENTS

INTRODUCTION

"Those who enjoy power always arrange matters so as to give their tyranny an appearance of justice." So wrote the French fableist La Fontaine in 1668. He could have been speaking of the great empires then being built, of British, French, Spanish, Portuguese and Dutch expansion, and later of German, Italian, and Japanese as well. Empire always seems to have mixed power, tyranny, and the desire for a just world in a way at once inextricable, confusing, and challenging.

"Imperialism" most readily is associated with Britain, primarily because she was so successful in building a vast empire that blanketed the globe and stretched at its height into every continent, covering the maps of the world with "cartographer's red." British imperialism was "imperialism *par excellence*." The study of imperialism, whether expanding or waning, "good" or "bad," must first of all be a study of the imperialism of a Greater Britain.

The word was virtually unknown, at least until comparatively late in the nineteenth century, to the imperialists themselves. *Imperialism* crept into the public ken from many sources, none of them initially sources that lay with the so-called imperialists. As late as 1878, well after imperialism is said to have entered its most expansive stage, Lord Carnarvon, Colonial Secretary in two Conservative British cabinets, wrote that he was "perplexed" by the "newly coined word." The term was meant to be abusive when used by Britain's enemies. Some thought it was given a kind of redemption by Rudyard Kipling and the trumpeters of the long British Processional who spoke of "white man's burden" as though it were a clearly defined kind of racial *noblesse oblige* and who talked of "the civilizing mission of the British race." With certainty the word now is one of abuse, a pejorative term synonomous with economic exploitation, racial prejudice, secret diplomacy, and war.

But the historian must not give to the Marxist economist a semantic victory. Imperialism was a human institution, presumably neither good nor bad save as administration, climate, and the will and purpose of human beings made it so. Today the word itself should be neutral, open to analysis, repair, or destruction at the hands of the scholar. Broad generalizations about imperialism will be very blunt instruments indeed for such delicate surgery.

The fact is that—whether Marxist or capitalist—we do not know nearly enough about the process called "imperialism" to be able, even yet, to arrive at more than tentative conclusions about the causes of imperial growth, the motivations of imperial leaders, or the effects of colonial administrations, either upon the colonial area or upon the imperial power. Yet, of course, ultimately the historian *must* generalize if he is not to remain an antiquarian, a grubber for small bits of string too short to use but too long to throw away.

Because "colonialism" still is a force in the world today, both as a term of immense propaganda value and as a reality for millions of Africans and Pacific Islanders, the nature of nineteenth-century British imperialism continues to pose many questions for the second half of the twentieth century. These questions range through two major groupings: those of cause and those of effect. What were the results of imperialism and of colonialism? An exploited people? An elevated people? An enriched people? What caused the Empire to rise? What caused the Empire to fall? Why did Britain extend its "protection"over Selangor, or the upper Niger, or the Fiji Islands? Between the breadth of the first questions and the specific nature of the last is a vast no man's land. Historians are closing in on this little-known land from below, as it were, while economists (and propagandists, who are free of the self-denying ordinance concerning the use of evidence that the historian must place upon himself) have been closing in from above. By now certain broad schools of thought have emerged, have been challenged, and have regrouped under the impact of such challenges. Most of the "causes" of imperialism have been identified; the chief source of historical controversy now turns on the priority to be given to these causes.

The so-called "new imperialism" after 1870, in particular, has been studied with care. Among the causes most frequently mentioned for the rapid growth of imperial holdings in the late nineteenth century are: the businessman's desire for quick and great profits; the psychological drive for power and mastery; the need, presumed or real, for raw materials and markets; the uncontrolled workings of an ill-understood economic system; the labor movement; naval tradition; a spirit of adventure; strategic and diplomatic considerations based upon an emerging sense of geopolitics; the rise of an inexpensive, sensation-seeking press; mass education; the growth of a bureaucratic civil service; the desire to save souls; the conviction of a mission to "civilize" the world; the search for God; and even the search for oneself. To be blind to any of these factors would be incredible, of course; to credit them all to equal degree is to be equally incredible. And so the historian will continue his research, the economist his analyses, and in the meantime the student will attempt, as all historians themselves must do, to arrive at a reasonable judgment upon the basis of the materials now at hand. The controversy over priority of causes will remain with us.

If any one generalization may stand, however, it is that British imperialism was based upon a sense of superiority, upon a conviction of a superior economic system, a superior political code, on access to a superior view of some Higher Being, on a superior way of life. Idealists and realists alike sought to spread what they felt in their hearts was superior, to spread their institutions *because* they were superior and therefore not only easy to spread but a positive good for those to whom they were applied—or a positive way to preserve the power and prestige of England, itself worth preserving at all costs because superior. The argument was circular, closed, complete. The British strategist, with no thought of God, could advocate annexation of a crucial peninsula because it controlled a strait that must, in turn, be controlled by the British Navy if the British were to prosper; the missionary, with thought only of God, could advocate annexation so that "pagans" might obtain the protection of a Christian nation, a nation superior because Christian.

Slaughter on evangelical principles is of course unique neither to the British nor to Christians. But abuse is inevitable in any situation that places the potential to unfettered power in the hands of those who consider themselves to represent a superior culture, for whatever reason. When fired by nationalism, and carried from the individual to the general, the nation, the conviction of actual or potential superiority leads to the desire for national dominance. In this way general questions relating to imperialism merge with broader and more pervasive questions concerning nationalism, love of nation, which itself supports both the noblest and the basest of ideas and actions. As Benjamin Disraeli instructed the readers of his novels through the figure of Sidonia in *Coningsby,* man must "Nurture [his] mind with great thoughts. To believe in the heroic makes heroes."

Those who have attempted to understand imperialism fall into three rough classifications: those who emphasize man's greed, his search for wealth, and the degree to which economic motivations dominate him; those who emphasize man's idealism, his desire to promote his vision of God, to create a better world, to express through his actions exalted and brave sentiments; and those who feel that nations and men are moved primarily by a quest for power, for personal and collective glory, by instincts both base and noble. The selections in this book are divided in approximately equal measure between the exponents and the critics of these three broad schools of thought. The old judgment that the Spanish *conquistadores* came to the New World in search of Glory, God, and Gold therefore continues to have meaning.

The first portion of the book consists of two classic statements on the economic causes of imperialism, together with two recent re-examinations of the economic arguments. The economic interpretation explains imperial expansion by the capitalist's need for new markets to absorb surplus industrial goods, his need to invest surplus or profit capital in undeveloped areas, and his need to acquire the sources of key raw materials essential to industrial growth. Since the exponents of the economic interpretation often agree in their analyses of imperialism while disagreeing in their analyses of the nature of capitalism and on the degree to which human beings can counter "economic laws," they have engaged in a series of family arguments—protracted debates over economic theory rather than over imperialism as such. One must always, therefore, give close attention to the nature of the questions the economic theorists have chosen to ask, as well as to the statistical data they assemble while outlining their answers.

The most important critic of imperial expansion from an economic viewpoint was an Englishman, J. A. Hobson, who published his influential study of *Imperialism* in 1902, when British expansion in Africa was at its zenith. He attributed imperialism to inherent weaknesses in the capitalist system and argued that a group of powerful financial leaders actually directed British policy from behind the scenes in order to find outlets for their surplus capital. Hobson was not blind to noneconomic problems, however, and for this reason his analysis is the single most important investigation of the causes of imperialism, an analysis that will be returned to time and again by other authors in this book.

V. I. Lenin found imperialism to be an inevitable and final stage of capitalism. He charged Hobson with "bourgeois social reformism," for Hobson felt that the capitalist system was capable of reformation. Lenin argued that the heart of imperialism was monopoly capitalism, a stage in the evolution of free competition, and that nothing could save capitalism from eventual decay from within, for the course of history was set, unalterable by any reforms within the capitalist system itself. The core of Marxist criticism of imperialism comes from Lenin's work, not from Karl Marx himself, since Marx died in 1883, well before modern imperial expansion had reached its highest stage.

In the next selections Mark Blaug, an economist, turns our attention to what he regards as serious historical and economic errors in Lenin's thesis, while an historian, D. K. Fieldhouse, submits Hobson in particular to analysis. He finds Hobson's statistics inadequate, his reasoning wayward, and the idea of sudden and vast discontinuity in history objectionable. Fieldhouse puts forward his own theory of imperialism, which places greater emphasis on personal and human factors than does the Marxist thesis of "economic man."

Hobson contended that imperialism was the work of a few powerful financiers operating behind the scenes. Then how does one explain the popular clamor for imperial expansion at the end of the century? Was this clamor spontaneous and natural or was it stimulated by these same financiers through the newspapers, the music halls, or even the educational institutions they controlled, as Hobson and Lenin assert? Four selections examine the nature of mass psychology as it relates to imperialism. Elie Halévy, a French historian who specialized in studies of nineteenth-century England, found imperialism was closely linked to the rise of labor, mass democracy, a broadening educational base, and inexpensive and sensational newspapers that catered to the newly educated and socially aspiring lower and middle classes. It is fitting that the Paris office of the *Times* of London, Britain's most powerful newspaper, should be on the *rue* Halévy, for the French historian placed particular emphasis on the way the press molded public opinion, leading rather than being led, creating a sense of national pride.

In selections that follow, A. P. Thornton and Walter E. Houghton single out, among many aspects of the problem, the nature of English public school education and the romantic adventure literature so popular at the time; while Gertrude Himmelfarb reveals how one highly intelligent and influential British author, John Buchan, could arrive at a personal philosophy of imperial responsibility. Halévy, Thornton, Houghton, and Himmelfarb argue, in effect, "Show me what a man reads and I will tell you what he is." An additional element in the creation of a popular sense of pride was racism, and a French sociologist, René Maunier, further argues that imperialism was rooted chiefly in man's desire for dominance, principally along racial lines.

Some writers, especially those of the economic school, discount public opinion on the grounds that small cliques secretly run a nation for their own benefit or that power elites shape opinion by controlling informational outlets. Other writers feel that democratic public opinion is a force which can make itself felt. What were the people reading? In addition to newspapers, schools, churches, and the music hall, from what sources did the people get their ideas? In the late nineteenth century, upper- and middle-class Britishers alike were thrilling to a renewed literature of romance.

So that the reader may assess for himself what both the masses and many among the educated elite were reading and hearing at the end of the nineteenth century, brief passages from popular literature, history, and science, and from political oratory, are included among the selections. Rudyard Kipling, in dozens of books, short stories, and poems, wrote of the glories of Britain, of "the white man's burden," and of the innocent savagery of a *Kim* or a Mowgli in *The Jungle Book*. His famous poem "If," which has inspired many teenagers to resolves of higher purpose, was written in virtual defense of one of the least defensible imperialists, Joseph Chamberlain. Kipling left no doubts about his sense of pride in what the British Empire had accomplished and could accomplish, and many must have joined with him in his famous toast of 1894, in "The Native-Born," to "the last and the largest Empire,/To the map that is half unrolled!"

H. Rider Haggard and G. A. Henty (who is not included among the readings) were, together with Sir Arthur Conan Doyle (and a little later, Buchan), the most popular novelists of the time, and hundreds of young empire builders were inspired to finish unrolling the imperial map as they tasted their first victories over Zulu or Watusi or Sikh warriors in the pages of Henty and Haggard. The latter's highly romantic tales of Africa, in particular *She* and *King Solomon's Mines,* left a lasting impression on all who read them. These writers were certain of their moral values, and so too were their readers. There was none of the confusing moral questioning of Graham Greene, none of the cynical harshness of Ian Fleming, and none of the implied glorification of the fortuitous as in Eric Ambler, three mid-twentieth-century authors who sometimes are thought to be descendents of the great Victorian tellers of tales. Issues were clear-cut and imperial responsibility was evident for all "right-minded people" to see.

God, the missionary impulse in man to convert others to his beliefs (or, more charitably, to do Christ's bidding by saving souls), also played an important part in expansion. Religion was a powerful motive force for hundreds of men who went to Africa and Asia to convert the pagan and who remained to hope for the protecting arm of a Protestant state. In two brief selections John S. Galbraith and George Bennett, an American and a British historian respectively, describe the attitudes of the missionaries and humanitarians.

Economic, political, social, and cultural values often were fused in a vision of Britain's mission for herself and for the world. The historian W. E. H. Lecky was one of the chief defenders of empire, arguing that Britain had a mission to mankind. The Irish-born author joined other scholars, notably J. R. Seeley, Regius Professor of Modern History at Cambridge, and J. A. Froude, who held the similar chair at Oxford, in seeing the empire as a result of historical evolution, divinely natural. Benjamin Kidd, like Herbert Spencer and Karl Pearson, found British superiority proved by the theories of Charles Darwin. Social Darwinists suggested that various societies patently were in different stages of evolutionary growth. Others, joining evolutionary theory with history, contended that growth and decay were natural to whole societies as they were to man and that the empire must continue to expand or it and then England would decay.

Kidd and popularizers like him were not racists. In *The Science of Power* (1918), published posthumously, he argued that when Negro children were schooled under the same conditions as European children, they would learn as readily. Thus the question was not one of "lesser breeds without the law," as Kipling wrote, but one of environmental conditions, the tacit assumption being made that the British environment was a superior one, one which should be exported to those who were less fortunate. Kidd's theories were widely held. By 1913 his *Social Evolution,* from which a selection is taken, had appeared in ten languages, including Chinese and Arabic; and he had repeated much the same arguments in another highly successful book, *The Control of the Tropics* (1898). But it was Chamberlain, stump speaker extraordinary, who could weave the assumptions of his more scientific colleagues into a rhetorical tapestry that was particularly convincing to the man-in-the-street, and the readings on the rhetoric of imperialism conclude with an extract from one of Chamberlain's most famous orations.

The third school of thought is neither materialist nor idealist but mixes the two in terms of both rational and irrational motives. A chief source of attack on the economic interpretation of imperialism comes, oddly enough, from an economist, Joseph A. Schumpeter. He considered imperialism to be a political and social atavism, an extension of the primitive past into the more progressive present, and thus emphasized the psychological factor in imperialism: man's desire for power. Capitalism, he concluded, was anti-imperialistic. While at times more emotional than analytical, at least in his terminology, Schumpeter's criticism has been an important one, by far the most influential attack on the economic interpretation yet written, in part because it comes from a member of the guild. In addition, Schumpeter offered an alternative hypothesis rather than restricting himself to the role of nay-sayer. Each man will have his nay-sayer nonetheless, and Murray Greene has played this role for the Schumpeter thesis, attacking the economist for having created highly specialized definitions of imperialism and capitalism and for then having struck down his own straw men.

Individual glory becomes national glory when elevated to national policy. Political and strategic motives for imperialism have more recently been given prominence. Several case studies have demonstrated that Britain annexed certain areas for fear that they would be acquired by a potential enemy and used as a base against legitimate British enterprises, or from concern that indigenous populations would engage in continued intertribal warfare to the detriment of their own and British activities, leading Britain to enter as a stabilizing force. Preventive annexation was not uncommon certainly, as studies of East Africa, Fiji, and New Zealand have shown, and the necessity to enter areas in order to bring about stability (and sometimes reluctantly to attempt to set right the overzealous and unauthorized activity of some local British official) was on occasion forced upon the Colonial Office, as new books on Malaya and India indicate. Such intervention was tied closely to events in European diplomacy, and Nicholas Mansergh argues, in the next selection, that certain leaders, especially in Germany, made specific diplomatic decisions, tied to the prevailing strategic concepts, that set in motion the ponderous machinery of imperial expansion.

K. M. Panikkar, a leading Asian historian, offers a highly controversial interpretation of the "Vasco de Gama epoch" in Asian history, in which he puts even greater stress than is now customary among European historians on the role of British sea power in imperial history and on the impact of one culture upon another, more ancient culture. Panikkar, in the selection printed here, attempts a kind of balance sheet on imperialism, assessing the benefits his native India has derived from British rule as well as the harm he feels was done to her. In particular he singles out, as enduring and beneficial aspects of British imperialism, the rule of law, the stimulus given to national sentiment, the growth of cities, and the impact of the English language and the new ideas borne with it. But he also is intensely critical of the arrogance, cruelty, and racism he finds associated with imperial growth.

It still is too early for the historian to assess with any high degree of accuracy the causes of and results from imperialism. Any modern balance sheet which is more than statistical must be impressionistic. It is, perhaps, symbolic that in 1884 an Empire Theatre was opened in Leicester Square in London and that today, only three-quarters of a century later, the stranger to London is not likely to be able to find even the square on his first attempt. But the time *has* come to reshape our questions. As Schumpeter has noted elsewhere, statistics help the historian to know what questions to ask; they do not provide him with his answers. A balance sheet will be interpretive and not statistical. In the final selection three younger British historians, Ronald Robinson, John Gallagher, and Alice Denny, re-examine the causes of imperialism in the light of recent scholarship, particularly about Africa, and conclude that Egypt and the Suez Canal are the pivotal points of imperial history, and that strategic and psychological factors were mixed in about equal proportion in British expansion. More important, however, is the evidence they provide that the task of interpretation involves a careful interweaving of all of the major theories of imperialism.

There can be as yet no balance sheet on imperialism. It is too much with us, too near, too controversial, too encumbered by closed archives and clouded by arguments, by past tensions relived, too obscured by the desire of men to make the past support their present purposes. But the historian and the student of history have the continuing obligation to keep asking, What caused imperialism? Was it beneficial or harmful? And why?*

*The selections deal only with the post-American Revolution period, and predominately with the period after 1870, since by historical convention the period before the Revolution is considered to relate to colonialism rather than to imperialism.

All but the most necessary explanatory footnotes have been eliminated by permission from the selections that follow.

THE CLASH OF OPINION

British Imperialism

Beneficial or Harmful?

"The central purpose of British colonial policy is simple. It is to guide the colonial territories to responsible self-government... in conditions that ensure to the people concerned both a fair standard of living and freedom from oppression in any quarter."

British Government *White Paper,* June 1948.

"Ruled by highly industrialized Britain, the overwhelming majority of the Indians lived in... unbelievable filth and squalor, reminiscent of the early Middle Ages... ill-housed, ill-clothed, and undernourished...."

Kumar Goshal, *People in Colonies* (New York, 1948).

"In many cases British colonial policy and administration have done for dependent territories what Point IV is designed to do for all tropical and other under-developed lands."

Sir Alan Burns, *In Defence of Colonies* (London, 1957).

"Imperialism has *always* been against the *general* interest of the working class."

Idris Cox, *Empire Today* (London, 1960).

Caused by Economic Need?

"... the dominant directive motive [behind imperialism] was the demand for markets and for profitable investment by the exporting and financial classes within each imperialist regime."

John A. Hobson, *Imperialism: A Study* (London, 1902).

"... it is clear that non-pecuniary motives have always loomed large in determining the flow of international capital."

Mark Blaug, "Economic Imperialism Revisited," *Yale Review* (March 1961).

"... imperialism ... must be characterised as capitalism in transition, or, more precisely, as dying capitalism."

V. I. Lenin, *Imperialism: The Highest Stage of Capitalism* (London, 1916).

"The only way you can fit history into what is roughly described as the economic or class interpretation is to leave out half or three-quarters of what happened and not ask any very bright questions about the remnant."

J. H. Hexter, *Reappraisals in History* (London, 1961).

Caused by a Love of God or a Search for Glory?

"The opening up of Africa was the work not of governments but of individuals possessed of great courage and remarkable powers of endurance... many of the explorers [being]... profoundly concerned with the welfare of the native races."

Nicholas Mansergh, *The Coming of the First World War* (London, 1949).

"Upon the maintenance of free communication in the Mediterranean depends... Great Britain's... support of her influence in the Levant... the air route to India, and the Kirkuk pipelines. Great Britain has always regarded the protection of the Suez Canal as a paramount duty.... Egypt is a focal point."

Royal Institute of International Affairs, *The Colonial Problem* (London, 1937).

"... imperialism owed its popular appeal not to the sinister influence of the capitalists, but to its inherent attractions for the masses."

D. K. Fieldhouse, "'Imperialism': An Historical Revision," *Economic History Review* (December 1961).

"It is now fairly clear... that the neo-Marxian critics have paid far too little attention to the imponderable, psychological ingredients of imperialism."

W. L. Langer, "A Critique of Imperialism," *Foreign Affairs* (October 1935).

In 1902 JOHN A. HOBSON (1858–1940), a British economist and journalist, wrote the most influential book on imperialism ever to appear. Any examination of the causes of imperial growth must begin with his *Imperialism: A Study*. Posing the fundamental question, Who benefits from imperialism?, Hobson gave the now classic answer associated with the economic interpretation: the investor, the munitions and arms manufacturer, the industrialist in search of markets, the capitalist with idle funds. Hobson argued that the basic weakness of capitalism was maldistribution of wealth and that imperialism enhanced this unequal distribution. His book was the result of a trip to South Africa for the *Manchester Guardian* shortly before the Boer War, which he opposed.*

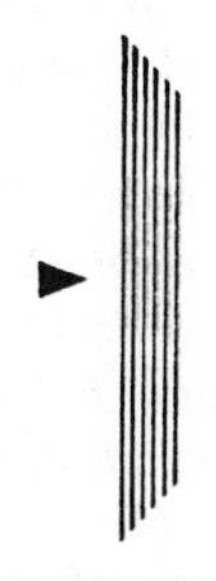

Imperialism: The Classic Statement

[W]hereas various real and powerful motives of pride, prestige and pugnacity, together with the more altruistic professions of a civilising mission, figured as causes of imperial expansion, the dominant directive motive was the demand for markets and for profitable investments by the exporting and financial classes within each imperialist regime. The urgency of this economic demand was attributed to the growing tendency of industrial productivity, under the new capitalist technique of machinery and power, to exceed the effective demand of the national markets, the rate of production to outrun the rate of home consumption. This was not, of course, the whole story. The rising productivity of industry required larger imports of some forms of raw materials, more imported foods for larger urban populations, and a great variety of imported consumption goods for a rising standard of living. These imports could only be purchased by a corresponding expansion of exports, or else by the incomes derived from foreign investments which implied earlier exports of capital goods.

But with these qualifications in mind, it is nevertheless true that the most potent drive towards enlarged export trade was the excess of capitalist production over the demands of the home market. . . . But when we find that at frequent inter-

* Excerpted and reprinted with permission of The Macmillan Company from *Imperialism: A Study* (rev. ed.; London, 1938), by John A. Hobson. Third edition first published in 1938 by George Allen and Unwin. Order of pages rearranged by permission.

vals there is a general excess of production beyond the current demands of the home and foreign markets, it becomes manifest that the productive power of capital has been excessively fed. This in its turn means that the processes of saving and investment have proceeded too rapidly. In other words there has been over-saving and under-spending....

[T]he constant impulse to push for overseas markets in normal times and the periodic slumps of national trade in the home markets, are due to a chronic tendency to try to save a larger proportion of the national income than can find a useful expression in new capital. This is not due to the folly of individual savers, but to a distribution of the general income which puts too small a share in the hands of the working-classes, too large a share in the hands of the employing and owning classes. For it is to the latter that over-saving is attributable....

...This drive towards oversaving is gradually checked by the inability of such saving to find any profitable use in the provision of more plant and other capital. But it also seeks to utilise political power for outlets in external markets, and as foreign independent markets are closed or restricted, the drive to the acquisition of colonies, protectorates and other areas of imperial development becomes a more urgent and conscious national policy. If this reasoning is correct, capitalism to maintain its profitable character, by utilising its new productive powers as fully as possible, is impelled to seek the help of the State in the various ways that are now so much in evidence, tariffs, embargoes, subsidies, and the acquisition or retention of colonies where the home capitalist can have advantages both for his import and export trade, with such securities in monetary matters as can be provided by imperial control....

[T]he various attempts to escape from the perils of excessive productivity... fall under three heads. One consists in the policy of organized labour and the State, aiming to secure a more equal and equitable distribution of the money and real income of the community by higher wages, shorter hours and other betterment of working and living conditions. The second consists in the business policy of restricted output... involving a close financial control of the major businesses in specified national or international industries, accompanied by a regulation of their markets and, when deemed desirable, by quotas and tariffs. The third method, and that most relevant to... Imperialism, is the combined or separate action of capital to obtain the help, financial, diplomatic, military, of the national government so as to secure preferential access to foreign markets and foreign areas of development by colonies, protectorates, spheres of preferential trade and other methods of a pushful economic foreign policy.... If, as many close investigators of the business world appear to hold, the capitalism which has prevailed for the past few centuries is in any case destined to disappear, it may seem better for its defenders to endeavour to prolong its life by political pressure for external markets than to succumb without a struggle to the popular demand for state socialism or a policy of social services, the expenses of which shall consume the whole of surplus profits....

It is not too much to say that the modern foreign policy of Great Britain has been primarily a struggle for profitable markets of investment. To a larger extent every year Great Britain has been becoming a nation living upon tribute from abroad, and the classes who enjoy this tribute have had an ever-increasing incentive to employ the public policy, the public purse, and the public force to extend the field of their private investments, and to safeguard and improve their existing investments....

What was true of Great Britain was true likewise of France, Germany, the United States, and of all countries in which modern capitalism had placed large surplus savings in the hands of a plutocracy or of a thrifty middle class. A well-recognised distinction is drawn between creditor and debtor countries. Great Britain had been for some time by far the largest creditor country, and the policy by which the investing classes used the instrument of the State for private business purposes is most richly illustrated in the history of her wars and annexations.... The nature of these imperialist operations is thus set forth by the Italian economist Loria.[1]

"When a country which has contracted a debt is unable, on account of the slenderness of its income, to offer sufficient guarantee for the punctual payment of interest, what happens? Sometimes an out-and-out conquest of the debtor country follows. Thus France's attempted conquest of Mexico during the second empire was undertaken solely with the view of guaranteeing the interest of French citizens holding Mexican securities. But more frequently the insufficient guarantee of an international loan gives rise to the appointment of a financial commission by the creditor countries in order to protect their rights and guard the fate of their invested capital. The appointment of such a commission literally amounts in the end, however, to a veritable conquest. We have examples of this in Egypt, which has to all practical purposes become a British province, and in Tunis, which has in like manner become a dependency of France, who supplies the greater part of the loan....

But, though useful to explain certain economic facts, the terms "creditor" and "debtor," as applied to countries, obscure the most significant feature of this Imperialism. For though ... much, if not most, of the debts were "public," the credit was nearly always private, though sometimes, as in the case of Egypt, its owners succeeded in getting their Government to enter a most unprofitable partnership, guaranteeing the payment of the interest, but not sharing in it.

Aggressive Imperialism, which costs the taxpayer so dear, which is of so little value to the manufacturer and trader, which is fraught with such grave incalculable peril to the citizen, is a source of great gain to the investor who cannot find at home the profitable use he seeks for his capital, and insists that his Government should help him to profitable and secure investments abroad.

If, contemplating the enormous expenditure on armaments, the ruinous wars, the diplomatic audacity or knavery by which modern Governments seek to extend their territorial power, we put the plain, practical question, *Cui bono?* the first and most obvious answer is, the investor....

The Measure of Imperialism

... During [the last sixty years] a number of European nations, Great Britain being first and foremost, annexed or otherwise asserted political sway over vast portions of Africa and Asia, and over numerous islands in the Pacific and elsewhere....

The following lists, giving the area and ... population of the new acquisi-

[1] Achille Loria, 1856-1943, a leading Italian economist and author of *The Economic Foundations of Society,* is best known in the United States for his influence on the theories of Richard T. Ely and Frederick Jackson Turner, the historian of the frontier. Hobson presumably came to know of Loria's work when, from 1896, Loria was the Italian correspondent of the Royal Economic Society of London—Ed.

tions, are designed to give definiteness to the term Imperialism. Though derived from official sources, they do not, however, profess strict accuracy. The sliding scale of political terminology along which no-man's land, or hinterland, passes into some kind of definite protectorate is often applied so as to conceal the process; "rectification" of a fluid frontier is continually taking place; paper "partitions" of spheres of influence or protection in Africa and Asia are often obscure, and in some cases the area and the population are highly speculative.

...The figures in the case of Great Britain are so startling as to call for a little further interpretation. I have thought it right to add to the recognized list of colonies and protectorates[2] the "veiled Protectorate" of Egypt, with its vast Soudanese claim, the entire territories assigned to Chartered Companies, and the native or feudatory States in India which acknowledged our paramountcy by the admission of a British Agent or other official endowed with real political control....

The list is by no means complete. It takes no account of several large regions which passed under the control of our Indian Government as native or feudatory States, but of which no statistics of area or population, even approximate were available. Such are the Shan States, the Burma Frontier, and the Upper Burma Frontier, the districts of Chitral, Bajam, Swat, Waziristan, which came under our "sphere of influence" in 1893, and have been since taken under a closer protectorate. The increase of British India itself between 1871 and 1891 amounted to an area of 104,993 square miles, with a population of 25,330,000, while no reliable measurement of the formation of new native States within that period and since is available. Many of the measurements here given are in round numbers, indicative of their uncertainty, but they are taken, wherever available, from official publications of the Colonial Office, corroborated or supplemented from the *Statesman's Year Book*.... [T]aken as they stand they make a formidable addition to the growth of an Empire whose nucleus is only 120,000 square miles, with 40,000,000 population.

For so small a nation to add to its domains in the course of a single generation an area of 4,754,000 square miles with an estimated population of 88,000,000, is a historical fact of great significance.

Accepting Sir Robert Giffen's[3] estimate of the size of our Empire (including Egypt and the Soudan) at about 13,000,000 square miles, with a population of some 400 to 420 millions (of whom about 50,000,000 are of British race and speech), we find that one-third of this Empire, containing quite one-fourth of the total population of the Empire, was acquired within the last thirty years of the nineteenth century....

The character of this Imperial expansion is clearly exhibited in the list of new territories.

Though, for convenience, the year 1870 has been taken as indicative of the beginning of a conscious policy of Imperialism, it will be evident that the movement did not attain its full impetus until the middle of the eighties. The vast increase of territory, and the method of wholesale partition which assigned to us great tracts of African land, may be dated from about 1884. Within fifteen years

[2] The Statistical Abstract for British Empire in 1903 (Cd. 2395, pub. 1905), gives an area of 9,631,100 sq. miles and a population of 360,646,000.

[3] Giffen was chief of the Board of Trade's statistical department—Ed.

	Date of Acquisition	Area Square Miles	Population
EUROPE—			
Cyprus	1878	3,584	237,022
AFRICA—			
Zanzibar and Pemba	1888	1,000,000	200,000
East Africa Protectorate	1895		2,500,000
Uganda Protectorate	1894–1896	140,000	3,800,000
Somali Coast Protectorate	1884–1885	68,000	(?)
British Central Africa Protectorate	1889	42,217	688,049
Lagos	to 1899	21,000	3,000,000
Gambia	to 1888	3,550	215,000
Ashantee	1896–1901	70,000	2,000,000
Niger Coast Protectorate	1885–1898	400,000 to 500,000	25,000,000 to 40,000,000
Egypt	1882	400,000	9,734,405
Egyptian Soudan	1882	950,000	10,000,000
Griqualand West	1871–1880	15,197	83,373
Zululand	1879–1897	10,521	240,000
British Bechuanaland	1885	51,424	72,736
Bechuanaland Protectorate	1891	275,000	89,216
Transkei	1879–1885	2,535	153,582
Tembuland	1885	4,155	180,130
Pondoland	1894	4,040	188,000
Griqualand East	1879–1885	7,511	152,609
British South Africa Charter	1889	750,000	321,000
Transvaal	1900	117,732	1,354,200
Orange River Colony	1900	50,000	385,045
ASIA—			
Hong Kong (littoral)	1898	376	102,284
Wei-hai-wei	—	270	118,000
Socotra	1886	1,382	10,000
Upper Burma	1887	83,473	2,046,933
Baluchistan	1876–1889	130,000	500,000
Sikkim	1890	2,818	30,000
Rajputana (States)	since 1881	128,022	12,186,352
Burma (States)		62,661	785,800
Jammu and Kashmir		80,000	2,543,952
Malay Protected States	1883–1895	24,849	620,000
North Borneo Co.	1881	31,106	175,000
North Borneo Protectorate	1888	—	—
Sarawak	1888	50,000	500,000
British New Guinea	1888	90,540	350,000
Fiji Islands	1874	7,740	120,124

some three and three-quarter millions of square miles were added to the British Empire.

Nor did Great Britain stand alone in this enterprise. The leading characteristic of that modern Imperialism, the competition of rival Empires, was the product of this same period. The close of the Franco-German war marked the beginning of a new colonial policy in France and Germany, destined to take effect in the next decade. It was not unnatural that the newly-founded German Empire, surrounded by powerful enemies and doubtful allies, and perceiving its more adventurous youth drawn into the United States and other foreign lands, should form the idea of a colonial empire. During the seventies a vigorous literature sprang up in advocacy of the policy which took shape a little latter in the powerful hands of Bismarck. The earliest instance of official aid for the promotion of German commerce abroad occurred in 1880 in the Government aid granted to the "German Commercial and Plantation Association of the Southern Seas." German connexion with Samoa dates from the same year, but the definite advance of Germany upon its imperialist career began in 1884, with a policy of African protectorates and annexations of Oceanic islands. During the next fifteen years she brought under her colonial sway about 1,000,000 square miles, with an estimated population of 14,000,000. Almost the whole of this territory was tropical, and the white population formed a total of a few thousands.

Similarly in France a great revival of the old colonial spirit took place in the early eighties, the most influential of the revivalists being the eminent economist, M. Paul Leroy-Beaulieu. The extension of empire in Senegal and Sahara in 1880 was followed next year by the annexation of Tunis, and France was soon actively engaged in the scramble for Africa in 1884, while at the same time she was fastening her rule on Tonking and Laos in Asia. Her acquisitions between 1880 and 1900 (exclusive of the extension of New Caledonia and its dependencies) amounted to an area of over three and a half million square miles, with a native population of some 37,000,000, almost the whole tropical or sub-tropical, inhabited by lower races and incapable of genuine French colonization. . . .

Russia, the only active expansionist country of the North, stood alone in the character of her imperial growth, which differed from other Imperialism in that it was principally Asiatic in its achievements and proceeded by direct extension of imperial boundaries, partaking to a larger extent than in the other cases of a regular colonial policy of settlement for purposes of agriculture and industry. It is, however, evident that Russian expansion, though of a more normal and natural order than that which characterises the new Imperialism, came definitely into contact and into competition with the claims and aspirations of the latter in Asia, and was advancing rapidly during the period. . . .

[R]ecent imperial expansion stands entirely distinct from the colonization of sparsely peopled lands in temperate zones, where white colonists carry with them the modes of government, the industrial and other arts of the civilization of the mother country. The "occupation" of these new territories was comprised in the presence of a small minority of white men, officials, traders, and industrial organisers, exercising political and economic sway over great hordes of population regarded as inferior and as incapable of exercising any considerable rights of self-government, in politics or industry.

The Commercial Value of Imperialism

The absorption of so large a proportion of public interest, energy, blood and money in seeking to procure colonial possessions and foreign markets would seem to indicate that Great Britain obtained her chief livelihood by external trade. Now this was not the case. Large as was our foreign and colonial trade in volume and in value, essential as was much of it to our national well-being, nevertheless it furnished a small proportion of the total industry of the nation.

According to the conjectural estimate of the Board of Trade "the proportion of the total labour of the British working classes which was concerned with the production of commodities for export (including the making of the instruments of this production and their transport to the ports) was between one-fifth and one-sixth of the whole."

If we suppose the profits, salaries, etc., in connexion with export trade to be at the same level with those derived from home trade, we may conclude that between one-fifth and one-sixth of the income of the nation comes from the production and carriage of goods for export trade.

Taking the higher estimate of the magnitude of foreign trade, we should conclude that it furnished employment to one-fifth of our industrial factors, the other four-fifths being employed in supplying home markets.

But this must not be taken as a measure of the net value of foreign trade to our nation, or of the amount of loss that would have been sustained by a diminution of our foreign markets. We are not entitled to assume that a tariff-policy or some other restrictive policy on the part of foreign nations which gradually reduced our export trade would imply an *equivalent* loss of national income, and of employment of capital and labour in Great Britain. The assumption, sometimes made, that home demand is a fixed amount, and that any commodities made in excess of this amount must find a foreign market, or remain unsold, is quite unwarranted. There is no necessary limit to the quantity of capital and labour that can be employed in supplying the home markets, provided the effective demand for the goods that are produced is so distributed that every increase of production stimulates a corresponding increase of consumption....

When a modern nation has attained a high level of development in those industrial arts which are engaged in supplying the first physical necessaries and conveniences of the population, an increasing proportion of her productive energies will begin to pass into higher kinds of industry, into the transport services, into distribution, and into professional, official and personal services, which produce goods and services less adapted on the whole for international trade than those simpler goods which go to build the lower stages of civilization. If this is true, it would appear that, whereas up to a certain point in the development of national life foreign trade will grow rapidly, after that point a decline, not in absolute size or growth but in relative size and growth, will take place....

Between 1870 and 1900,... the value of our foreign trade had not grown so fast as our population. Whereas upon the generally accepted estimate the growth of the income of the nation during these three decades was from about £1,200,000,000 to £1,750,000,000, yielding an increase of about 10 per cent. in the income per head of the population, the value of foreign trade per head had positively shrunk....

Annual Averages	Imports into Great Britain from		Exports from Great Britain to	
	Foreign Countries	British Possessions	Foreign Countries	British Possessions
1855–1859	76.5	23.5	68.5	31.5
1860–1864	71.2	28.8	66.6	33.4
1865–1869	76.0	24.0	72.4	27.6
1870–1874	78.0	22.0	74.4	25.6
1875–1879	77.9	22.1	67.0	33.0
1880–1884	76.5	23.5	65.5	34.5
1885–1889	77.1	22.9	65.0	35.0
1890–1894	77.1	22.9	66.5	33.5
1895–1899	78.4	21.6	66.0	34.0
1900–1903	77.3	20.7	63.0	37.0

This table (Cd. 1761 p. 407) refers to merchandise only, excluding bullion. From the export trade, ships and boats (not recorded prior to 1897) are excluded. In exports British produce alone is included....

Next, let us inquire whether the vast outlay of energy and money upon imperial expansion was attended by a growing trade within the Empire as compared with foreign trade. In other words, does the policy tend to make us more and more an economically self-sufficing Empire? Does trade follow the flag?

The figures in the table [above]... represent the proportion which our trade with our colonies and possessions bears to our foreign trade during the last half of the nineteenth century.

A longer period is here taken as a basis of comparison in order to bring out clearly the central truth, viz., that Imperialism had no appreciable influence whatever on the determination of our external trade until the protective and preferential measures taken during and after the Great War. Setting aside the abnormal increase of exports to our colonies in 1900–1903 due to the Boer War, we perceive that the proportions of our external trade had changed very little during the half century; colonial imports slightly fell, colonial exports slightly rose, during the last decade, as compared with the beginning of the period. Although since 1870 such vast additions have been made to British possessions, involving a corresponding reduction of the area of "Foreign Countries," this imperial expansion was attended by no increase in the proportions of intra-imperial trade as represented in the imports and exports of Great Britain during the nineteenth century.

From the standpoint of the recent history of British trade there is no support for the dogma that "Trade follows the Flag."...

Imperialism as an Outlet for Population

There is a widely prevalent belief that imperial expansion is desirable, or even necessary, in order to absorb and utilize the surplus of our ever-growing population. "The reproductive powers of nature," runs the argument, "brook no restraint: the most dominant force in history is the tendency of population to overflow its ancient banks, seeking fuller and easier subsistence. Great Britain is one of the most congested areas in the world; her growing population cannot find enough remunerative occupation within these islands; professional and working-classes alike find it more and more difficult to earn a decent and secure living, every labour market is overstocked, emigration is a prime economic necessity.... It is our most urgent national interest that this surplus emigrant population shall settle in lands which are under the British flag, and we must therefore maintain a constant policy of extending the political control of Great Britain so as to cover the new homes to which these people betake themselves in pursuit of employment." This motive is closely linked with other economic motives relating to trade and investments. The establishment of British trade, and especially of British capital, in foreign lands naturally attracts a certain British population; traders, engineers, overseers, and mechanics are needed as entrepreneurs and managers. So wherever a new area was opened up to our trade and capital the nucleus of an outlander population was formed. Hence, of necessity, sprang up a crop of political issues, an outlander problem: the British outlanders, not satisfied with the foreign rule, demanded the intervention of their home Government....

Such has been the accepted theory and practice. What validity did it possess as an argument for imperial expansion? Let me first ask: Was England over-populated, and was the prospect of further increase such as to compel us to "peg our claims for posterity" in other parts of the world? The facts are these. Great Britain is not and was not so thickly populated as certain prosperous industrial areas in Germany, the Netherlands, and China: along with every recent growth of population has come a far greater growth of wealth and of the power to purchase food and other subsistence. The modern specialization of industry has caused a congestion of population upon certain spots which may be injurious in some ways to the well-being of the nation, but it cannot be regarded as over-population in the sense of a people outgrowing the means of subsistence....

The total emigration of Britons represents no large proportion of the population; that proportion during the years of imperial expansion perceptibly diminished: of the emigrants less than one-half settled in British possessions, and an infinitesimally small fraction settled in the countries acquired under the new Imperialism....

Economic Parasites of Imperialism

Seeing that the Imperialism of the last six decades is clearly condemned as a business policy, in that at enormous expense it has procured a small, bad, unsafe increase of markets, and has jeopardised the entire wealth of the nation in rousing the strong resentment of other nations, we may ask, "How is the British nation induced to embark upon such unsound business?" The only possible answer is that the business interests of the nation as a whole are subordinated to those of certain sectional interests that usurp control of the national resources and use them for their private gain. This is no strange or monstrous charge to bring; it is the commonest disease of all forms of government....

Although the new Imperialism has been bad business for the nation, it has been good business for certain classes and certain trades within the nation. The vast expenditure on armaments, the costly wars, the grave risks and embarrassments of foreign policy, the checks upon political and social reforms within Great Britain, though fraught with great injury to the nation, have served well the present business interests of certain industries and professions....

In order to explain Imperialism on this hypothesis we have to answer two questions. Do we find in Great Britain any well-organised group of special commercial and social interests which stand to gain by aggressive Imperialism and the militarism it involves? If such a combination of interests exists, has it the power to work its will in the arena of politics?

What is the direct economic outcome of Imperialism? A great expenditure of public money upon ships, guns, military and naval equipment and stores, growing and productive of enormous profits when a war, or an alarm of war, occurs; new public loans and important fluctuations in the home and foreign Bourses; more posts for soldiers and sailors and in the diplomatic and consular services; improvement of foreign investments by the substitution of the British flag for a foreign flag; acquisition of markets for certain classes of exports, and some protection and assistance for British trades in these manufactures; employment for engineers, missionaries, speculative miners, ranchers and other emigrants.

Certain definite business and professional interests feeding upon imperialistic expenditure, or upon the results of that expenditure, are thus set up in opposition to the common good, and, instinctively feeling their way to one another, are found united in strong sympathy to support every new imperialist exploit.

If the £60,000,000 which may now be taken as a minimum expenditure on armaments in time of peace was subjected to a close analysis, most of it would be traced directly to the tills of certain big firms engaged in building warships and transports, equipping and coaling them, manufacturing guns, rifles, ammunition, 'planes and motor vehicles of every kind, supplying horses, waggons, saddlery, food, clothing for the services, contracting for barracks, and for other large irregular needs. Through these main channels the millions flow to feed many subsidiary trades, most of which are quite aware that they are engaged in executing contracts for the services. Here we have an important nucleus of commercial Imperialism....

These men are Imperialists by conviction; a pushful policy is good for them.

With them stand the great manufacturers for export trade, who gain a living by supplying the real or artificial wants of the new countries we annex or open up. Manchester, Sheffield, Birmingham, to name three representative cases, are full of firms which compete in pushing textiles and hardware, engines, tools, machinery, spirits, guns, upon new markets. The public debts which ripen in our colonies, and in foreign countries that come under our protectorate or influence, are largely loaned in the shape of rails, engines, guns, and other materials of civilization made and sent out by British firms. The making of railways, canals, and other public works, the establishment of factories, the development of mines, the improvement of agriculture in new countries, stimulate a definite interest in important manufacturing industries which feed a very firm imperialist faith in their owners....

The shipping trade has a very definite interest which makes for Imperialism. This is well illustrated by the policy of State subsidies now claimed by shipping firms as a retainer, and in order to encourage British shipping for purposes of imperial safety and defence.

The services are, of course, imperialist by conviction and by professional interest, and every increase of the army, navy and air force enhances the political power they exert. The abolition of purchase in the army, by opening the profession to the upper middle classes, greatly enlarged this most direct feeder of imperial sentiment. The potency of this factor is, of course, largely due to the itch for glory and adventure among military officers upon disturbed or uncertain frontiers of the Empire. This has been a most prolific source of expansion in India. The direct professional influence of the services carries with it a less organised but powerful sympathetic support on the part of the aristocracy and the wealthy classes, who seek in the services careers for their sons. . . .

From this standpoint our colonies still remain what James Mill cynically described them as being, "a vast system of outdoor relief for the upper classes.". . .

By far the most important economic factor in Imperialism is the influence relating to investments. The growing cosmopolitanism of capital has been the greatest economic change of recent generations. Every advanced industrial nation has been tending to place a larger share of its capital outside the limits of its own political area, in foreign countries, or in colonies, and to draw a growing income from this source.

No exact or even approximate estimate of the total amount of the income of the British nation derived from foreign investments is possible. We possess, however, in the income tax assessments an indirect measurement of certain large sections of investments, from which we can form some judgment as to the total size of the income from foreign and colonial sources, and the rate of its growth. . . .

Sir R. Giffen estimated the income derived from foreign sources as profit, interest and pensions in 1882 at £70,000,000, and in . . . 1899 he estimated the income from the same sources for the current year at £90,000,000. It is probable that this last figure is an underestimate, for if the items of foreign income not included as such under the income-tax returns bear the same proportion to those included as in 1882, the total of income from foreign and colonial investments should be £120,000,000 rather than £90,000,000. Sir R. Giffen hazarded the calculation that the new public investments abroad in the sixteen years 1882–1898 amounted to over £800,000,000, "and though part of the sum may have been nominal only, the real investment must have been enormous.". . .

[I]n 1893 the British capital invested abroad represented about 15 per cent. of the total wealth of the United Kingdom; nearly one-half of this capital was in the form of loans to foreign and colonial Governments; of the rest a large proportion was invested in railways, banks, telegraphs, and other public services, owned, controlled, or vitally affected by Governments, while most of the remainder was placed in lands and mines, or in industries directly dependent on land values.

Income tax returns and other statistics descriptive of the growth of . . . investments indicate that the total amount of British investments abroad at the end of the nineteenth century cannot be set down at a lower figure than [£2,000,000,000]. . . . Considering that . . . Giffen regarded as "moderate" the estimate of £1,700,000,000 in 1892, the figure here named is probably below the truth.

Now, without placing any undue reliance upon these estimates, we cannot fail to recognise that in dealing with these foreign investments we are facing the most important factor in the economics of Imperialism. Whatever figures we take, two facts are evident. First, that the income derived as interest upon foreign investments enormously exceeded that derived as profits upon ordinary export and import trade. Secondly, that while our foreign and colonial trade, and presumably the income from it, were growing but slowly, the share of our import values representing income from foreign investments was growing very rapidly.

...The statistics of foreign investments ... shed clear light upon the economic forces which dominate our policy. While the manufacturing and trading classes make little out of their new markets, paying, if they knew it, much more in taxation than they get out of them in trade, it is quite otherwise with the investor....

The annual income Great Britain derives from commissions on her whole foreign and colonial trade, import and export, was estimated by ... Giffen at £18,000,000 for 1899, taken at 2½ per cent., upon a turnover of £800,000,000. This is the whole that we are entitled to regard as profits on external trade. Considerable as this sum is, it cannot serve to yield an economic motive-power adequate to explain the dominance which business considerations exercise over our imperial policy. Only when we set beside it some £90,000,000 or £100,000,000, representing pure profit upon investments, do we understand whence the economic impulse to Imperialism is derived....

If the special interest of the investor is liable to clash with the public interest and to induce a wrecking policy, still more dangerous is the special interest of the financier, the general dealer in investments. In large measure the rank and file of the investors are, both for business and for politics, the cat'spaws of the great financial houses, who use stocks and shares not so much as investments to yield them interest, but as material for speculation in the money market. In handling large masses of stocks and shares, in floating companies, in manipulating fluctuations of values, the magnates of the Bourse find their gain. These great businesses—banking, broking, bill discounting, loan floating, company promoting—form the central ganglion of international capitalism. United by the strongest bonds of organisation, always in closest and quickest touch with one another, situated in the very heart of the business capital of every State, controlled, so far as Europe is concerned, chiefly by men of a single and peculiar race, who have behind them many centuries of financial experience, they are in a unique position to manipulate the policy of nations. No great quick direction of capital is possible save by their consent and through their agency. Does any one seriously suppose that a great war could be undertaken by any European State, or a great State loan subscribed, if the house of Rothschild and its connexions set their face against it? ...

The wealth of these houses, the scale of their operations, and their cosmopolitan organisation make them the prime determinants of imperial policy. They have the largest definite stake in the business of Imperialism, and the amplest means of forcing their will upon the policy of nations.

In view of the part which the non-economic factors of patriotism, adventure, military enterprise, political ambition, and philanthropy play in imperial expansion, it may appear that to impute to financiers so much power is to take a too narrowly economic view of history. And it is true that the motor-power of Imperialism is not chiefly financial: finance is rather the governor of the imperial engine, directing the energy and determining its work: it does not constitute the fuel of the engine, nor does it directly generate the power. Finance manipulates the patriotic forces which politicians, soldiers, philanthropists, and traders generate; the enthusiasm for expansion which issues from these sources, though strong and genuine, is irregular and blind; the financial interest has those qualities of concentration and clear-sighted calculation which are needed to set Imperialism to work. An ambitious statesman, a frontier soldier, an over-zealous missionary, a pushing trader, may suggest or even initiate a step of imperial expansion, may assist in educating patriotic public opinion to the urgent need of some fresh advance, but the final determination rests with the financial power. The direct influence exercised by great financial houses in "high politics" is supported by the control which they exercise over the body of public opinion through the Press, which, in every "civilised" country, is becoming more and more their obedient instrument.... In Berlin, Vienna, and Paris many of the influential newspapers have been held by financial houses, which used them, not primarily to make direct profits out of them, but in order to put into the public mind beliefs and sentiments which would influence public policy and thus affect the money market.... Apart from the financial Press, and financial ownership of the general Press, the City has notoriously exercised a subtle and abiding influence upon leading London newspapers, and through them upon the body of the provincial Press, while the entire dependence of the Press for its business profits upon its advertising columns has involved a peculiar reluctance to oppose the organised financial classes with whom rests the control of so much advertising business. Add to this the natural sympathy with a sensational policy which a cheap Press always manifests, and it becomes evident that the Press has been strongly biased towards Imperialism, and has lent itself with great facility to the suggestion of financial or political Imperialists who have desired to work up patriotism for some new piece of expansion....

The Economic Taproot of Imperialism

No mere array of facts and figures adduced to illustrate the economic nature of the new Imperialism will suffice to dispel the popular delusion that the use of national force to secure new markets by annexing fresh tracts of territory is a sound and a necessary policy for an advanced industrial country like Great Britain. It has indeed been proved that recent annexations of tropical countries, procured at great expense, have furnished poor and precarious markets, that our aggregate trade with our colonial possessions is virtually stationary, and that our most profitable and progressive trade is with rival industrial nations, whose territories we have no desire to annex, whose markets we cannot force, and whose active antagonism we are provoking by our expansive policy.

But these arguments are not conclusive. It is open to Imperialists to argue thus: "We must have markets for our growing manufactures, we must have new outlets for the investment of our surplus capital and for the energies of the adventurous surplus of our population: such expansion is a necessity of life to a nation with our great and growing powers of production. An ever larger share of our population is devoted to the manufactures and commerce of towns, and is thus dependent for life and work upon food and raw materials from foreign lands. In order to buy and pay for these things we must sell our goods abroad. During the first three-quarters of the nineteenth century we could do so without difficulty by a natural expansion of commerce with continental nations and our colonies, all of which were far behind us in the main arts of manufacture and the carrying trades. So long as England held a virtual monopoly of the world markets for certain important classes of manufactured goods, Imperialism was unnecessary. After 1870 this manufacturing and trading supremacy was greatly impaired: other nations, especially Germany, the United States, and Belgium, advanced with great rapidity, and while they have not crushed or even stayed the increase of our external trade, their competition made it more difficult to dispose of the full surplus of our manufactures at a profit. The encroachments made by these nations upon our old markets, even in our own possessions, made it most urgent that we should take energetic means to secure new markets. These new markets had to lie in hitherto undeveloped countries, chiefly in the tropics, where vast populations lived capable of growing economic needs which our manufacturers and merchants could supply. Our rivals were seizing and annexing territories for similar purposes, and when they had annexed them closed them to our trade. The diplomacy and the arms of Great Britain had to be used in order to compel the owners of the new markets to deal with us: and experience showed that the safest means of securing and developing such markets is by establishing 'protectorates' or by annexation. The value in 1905 of these markets must not be taken as a final test of the economy of such a policy; the process of educating civilized needs which we can supply is of necessity a gradual one, and the cost of such Imperialism must be regarded as a capital outlay, the fruits of which posterity would reap. The new markets might not be large, but they formed serviceable outlets for the overflow of our great textile and metal industries, and, when the vast Asiatic and African populations of the interior were reached, a rapid expansion of trade was expected to result.

"Far larger and more important is the pressure of capital for external fields of investment. Moreover, while the manufacturer and trader are well content to trade with foreign nations, the tendency for investors to work towards the political annexation of countries which contain their more speculative investments is very powerful. Of the fact of this pressure of capital there can be no question. Large savings are made which cannot find any profitable investment in this country; they must find employment elsewhere, and it is to the advantage of the nation that they should be employed as largely as possible in lands where they can be utilized in opening up markets for British trade and employment for British enterprise.

"However costly, however perilous, this process of imperial expansion may be, it is necessary to the continued existence and progress of our nation; if we abandoned it we must be content to leave the development of the world to other nations, who will everywhere cut into our trade, and even impair our means of securing the food and raw materials we require to support our population. Imperialism is thus seen to be, not a choice, but a necessity."

The practical force of this economic argument in politics is strikingly illustrated by the later history of the United States. Here is a country which suddenly broke through a conservative policy, strongly held by both political parties, bound up with every popular instinct and tradition, and flung itself into a rapid imperial career for which it possessed neither the material nor the moral equipment, risking the principles and practices of liberty and equality by the establishment of militarism and the forcible subjugation of peoples which it could not safely admit to the condition of American citizenship. . . .

. . . American Imperialism was the natural product of the economic pressure of a sudden advance of capitalism which could not find occupation at home and needed foreign markets for goods and for investments.

The same needs existed in European countries, and, as is admitted, drove Governments along the same path. Overproduction in the sense of an excessive manufacturing plant, and surplus capital which could not find sound investments within the country, forced Great Britain, Germany, Holland, France to place larger and larger portions of their economic resources outside the area of their present political domain, and then stimulate a policy of political expansion so as to take in the new areas. . . .

The process, we may be told, is inevitable, and so it seems upon a superficial inspection. Everywhere appear excessive powers of production, excessive capital in search of investment. It is admitted by all business men that the growth of the powers of production in their country exceeds the growth in consumption, that more goods can be produced than can be sold at a profit, and that more capital exists than can find remunerative investment.

It is this economic condition of affairs that forms the taproot of Imperialism. If the consuming public in this country raised its standard of consumption to keep pace with every rise of productive powers, there could be no excess of goods or capital clamorous to use Imperialism in order to find markets. . . .

But it may be asked, "Why should there be any tendency to over-savings? Why should the owners of consuming power withhold a larger quantity for savings than can be serviceably employed?" Another way of putting the same question is this, "Why should not the pressure of present wants keep pace with every possibility of satisfying them?" The answer to these pertinent questions carries us to the broadest issue of the distribution of wealth. If a tendency to distribute income or consuming power according to needs were operative, it is evident that consumption would rise with every rise of producing power, for human needs are illimitable, and there could be no excess of saving. But it is quite otherwise in a state of economic society where distribution has no fixed relation to needs, but is determined by other conditions which assign to some people a consuming power vastly in excess of needs or possible uses, while others are destitute of consuming power enough to satisfy even the full demands of physical efficiency. . . .

The fallacy of the supposed inevitability of imperial expansion as a necessary outlet for progressive industry is now manifest. It is not industrial progress that demands the opening up of new markets and areas of investment, but maldistribution of consuming power which prevents the absorption of commodities and capital within the country. . . .

The struggle for markets, the greater eagerness of producers to sell than of consumers to buy, is the crowning proof of a false economy of distribution. Imperialism is the fruit of this false economy; "social reform" is its remedy. The primary purpose of "social reform," using the term in its economic signification, is to raise the wholesome standard of private and public consumption for a nation, so as to enable the nation to live up to its highest standard of production.

Writing *Imperialism: The Highest Stage of Capitalism* while in exile in Switzerland in 1916, V. I. LENIN (1870–1924), carried the theories of Hobson and of the Austrian "Neo-Marxist" economist, Rudolph Hilferding, to their logical Marxist conclusion. Soon to be the victorious Communist leader of the Russian Revolution, the chief theorist of modern communism wrote this book partly as an economic analysis and partly as a campaign tract, as it were, to justify his intended political program. On the various factions within the general Marxist framework, the reader should consult Earl Winslow's article, "Marxian, Liberal, and Sociological Theories of Imperialism," in *The Journal of Political Economy,* XXXIX (December 1931), 713–758.*

Imperialism: The Highest Stage of Capitalism

Imperialism as a Special Stage of Capitalism

Imperialism emerged as a development and direct continuation of the fundamental properties of capitalism in general. But capitalism became capitalist imperialism only at a definite, very high stage of its development, when certain of its fundamental properties had begun to change into their opposites, when the features of a period of transition from capitalism to a higher socio-economic system had begun to take shape and reveal themselves all along the line. Economically fundamental in this process is the replacement of capitalist free competition by capitalist monopolies. . . .

If it were necessary to give the briefest possible definition of imperialism, we should have to say that imperialism is the monopoly stage of capitalism. Such a definition would include the essential point, for, on the one hand, finance capital is bank capital of the few biggest monopolist banks, merged with the capital of the monopolist combines of industrialists; on the other hand, the division of the world is the transition from a colonial policy which has extended without hindrance to territories unoccupied by any capitalist power, to a colonial policy of monopolistic possession of the territories of the world, which has been completely divided up.

But too brief definitions, although

* Excerpted from V. I. Lenin, *Imperialism: The Highest Stage of Capitalism* (rev. trans., 2d ed.; New York, 1934).

convenient, since they sum up the main points, are neverthless inadequate, because very fundamental features of the phenomenon to be defined must still be deduced. And so, without forgetting the conditional and relative value of all definitions, which can never include all the connections of a fully developed phenomenon, we must give a definition of imperialism that will include the following five essential features:

1. The concentration of production and capital, developed to such a high stage that it has created monopolies which play a decisive rôle in economic life.
2. The merging of bank capital with industrial capital and the creation, on the basis of this "finance capital," of a financial oligarchy.
3. The export of capital, as distinguished from the export of commodities, becomes of particularly great importance.
4. International monopoly combines of capitalists are formed which divide up the world.
5. The territorial division of the world by the greatest capitalist powers is completed....

In defining imperialism, ... we have to enter into controversy, primarily, with Karl Kautsky, the principal Marxist theoretician of the epoch of the so-called Second International—that is, of the twenty-five years between 1889 and 1914.

Kautsky, in 1915 and even in November, 1914, decisively attacked the fundamental ideas expressed in our definition of imperialism. He declared that imperialism must not be regarded as a "phase" or as an economic stage, but as a policy....

Kautsky's definition is as follows:

> Imperialism is a product of highly developed industrial capitalism. It consists in the striving of every industrial capitalist nation to bring under its control and to annex larger and larger *agrarian* [Kautsky's italics] regions, irrespective of what nations inhabit them.

This definition is utterly worthless because it is one-sided, *i.e.,* it arbitrarily brings out the national question alone (admittedly, it is extremely important in itself as well as in its relation to imperialism); arbitrarily and *incorrectly* it connects this question *only* with the industrial capital in the countries which annex other nations; in an equally arbitrary and incorrect manner it emphasises the annexation of agrarian regions.

Imperialism is a striving for annexations—this is what the *political* part of Kautsky's definition amounts to. It is correct, but very incomplete, for politically, imperialism is generally a striving towards violence and reaction. We are interested here, however, in the *economic* aspect of the question, which Kautsky *himself* introduced into *his own* definition. The errors in the definition of Kautsky are clearly evident. The characteristic feature of imperialism is *not* industrial capital, *but* finance capital. It is not an accident that in France, it was precisely the extraordinarily rapid development of *finance* capital and the weakening of industrial capital, that, from 1880 onwards, gave rise to a sharpening of annexationist (colonial) policy. The characteristic feature of imperialism is precisely the fact that it strives to annex *not only* agrarian but even the most industrialised regions (the German appetite for Belgium; the French appetite for Lorraine), first, because the fact that the world is already partitioned makes it necessary, in the event of a *re-partition,* to stretch out one's hand to *any* kind of territory, and second, because an essential feature of imperialism is the rivalry between a number of great powers in striving for hegemony, *i.e.,* for the seizure of territory, not so much for their own direct advantage as to weaken the adversary and undermine *his* hegemony....

...We see that Kautsky, while pretending that he is continuing to defend Marxism, is really taking a step backward in comparison with the *social-liberal* Hobson, who rightly takes account of two "historically concrete"... features of modern imperialism: (1) the competition between *several* imperialisms and (2) the predominance of the financier over the merchant. Yet if it were chiefly a question of the annexation of an agrarian country by an industrial one, the rôle played by the merchant would be predominant.

But Kautsky's definition is not only wrong and un-Marxian. It serves as a basis for a whole system of views which all along the line run counter to Marxian theory and practise.... The important thing is that Kautsky detaches the policy of imperialism from its economics, speaks of annexations as being a policy "preferred" by finance capital, and opposes to it another bourgeois policy which he alleges to be possible on the same basis of finance capital.... The result is a slurring-over and a blunting of the most profound contradictions of the newest stage of capitalism, instead of an exposure of their depth. The result is bourgeois reformism instead of Marxism....

The question as to whether it is possible to change the bases of imperialism by reforms, whether to go forward to a further aggravation and accentuation of the contradictions it engenders, or backwards towards allaying them, is a fundamental question in the critique of imperialism. The fact that the political characteristics of imperialism are reaction all along the line and increased national oppression, in connection with oppression by the financial oligarchy and the elimination of free competition, has given rise to a petty-bourgeois-democratic opposition to imperialism in almost all imperialist countries since the beginning of the twentieth century. And the break with Marxism made by Kautsky and the broad international Kautskyist tendency consists in the very fact that Kautsky not only did not trouble to, and did not know how to, take a stand against this petty-bourgeois reformist opposition, which is reactionary in its economic basis, but, on the contrary, in practice became identified with it.

For Britain, the period of vast increase in colonial conquests falls between 1860 and 1880; and the last twenty years of the nineteenth century are also of great importance. For France and Germany it falls precisely during those last twenty years.... [T]he apex of pre-monopoly capitalist development, of capitalism in which free competition was predominant, was reached in the period between 1860 and 1880. We now see that it is *precisely after that period* that the tremendous "boom" in colonial annexations begins, and that the struggle for a territorial division of the world becomes extraordinarily keen. It is beyond doubt, therefore, that the transition of capitalism to the stage of monopoly capitalism, to finance capital, is *connected* with the intensification of the struggle for the partition of the world....

Between 1840 and 1860, when free competition in England was at its height, the leading bourgeois politicians were *opposed* to the colonial policy, and were of the opinion that the liberation of the colonies and their complete separation from England was an inevitable and desirable thing.... [I]n 1852, Disraeli, a statesman generally inclined towards imperialism, declared: "The colonies are millstones round our necks." But by the end of the nineteenth century, the heroes of the hour were Cecil Rhodes and Joseph Chamberlain, the open advocates of imperialism and the most cynical exponents of imperialist policy!

It is not without interest to observe that already at that time the leading British bourgeois politicians fully appreciated the connection between what might be called the purely economic and the social-political roots of modern imperialism. Chamberlain preached imperialism as the "true, wise and economical policy," and he pointed particularly to the German, American and Belgian competition which Great Britain to-day encounters on the world market. Salvation lies in monopolies, said the capitalists, as they formed cartels, syndicates and trusts. Salvation lies in monopolies, echoed the political leaders of the bourgeoisie, hastening to seize the parts of the world not yet partitioned....

The basic feature of the newest capitalism is the domination of monopolist combines of the biggest entrepreneurs. These monopolies are most durable when *all* the sources of raw materials are controlled by the one group.... Colonial possession alone gives a complete guarantee of success to the monopolies against all the risks of the struggle against competitors, including the possibility of the adversary's desire to defend himself by means of a law establishing a state monopoly. The more capitalism develops, the more the need for raw materials is felt; the more bitter competition becomes and the more feverish the hunt for sources of raw materials throughout the world, the more desperate the struggle for the acquisition of colonies becomes....

The bourgeois reformists, and among them particularly the present-day Kautskyists, of course, try to belittle the importance of facts of this kind by arguing that it "would be possible" to obtain raw materials in the open market without a "costly and dangerous" colonial policy; and that it would be "possible" greatly to increase the supply of raw materials "simply" by improving agricultural conditions in general. But such arguments degenerate into an apology for imperialism, into beautifying it, for they are based on disregard of the principal characteristic of the newest capitalism: monopoly. Free markets are becoming more and more a thing of the past; monopolist syndicates and trusts are cutting into them more and more every day, and "simply" improving agricultural conditions resolves itself into improving the conditions of the masses, raising wages and reducing profits....

We have seen that by its economic essence imperialism is monopolist capitalism. This fact alone determines the place of imperialism in history, for monopoly growing up on the basis of free competition, and precisely out of free competition, is the transition from the capitalist to a higher social economic order. We must take special note of four main aspects of monopolies, or principal manifestations of monopoly capitalism, which are characteristic of the period under discussion.

First, monopoly arose out of the concentration of production at a very high stage of development. This refers to the monopolist capitalist combines: cartels, syndicates and trusts. We have seen the important part they play in modern economic life. Towards the beginning of the twentieth century, they acquired complete supremacy in the advanced countries, and although the initial steps towards the formation of combines were first taken by countries with high protective tariffs (Germany, America), Great Britain, with her system of free trade, was not far behind in revealing the same fundamental fact, namely, the birth of monopolies out of the concentration of production.

Second, monopolies have accelerated seizure of the most important sources of raw materials, especially for the coal and iron industry, which is the basic and most highly trustified industry in capitalist society. The monopolistic control of the most important sources of raw materials has enormously increased the power of big capital, and has sharpened the antagonism between trustified and non-trustified industry.

Third, monopoly arose out of the banks. The banks changed from modest intermediary enterprises into the monopolists of finance capital. Some three or five of the biggest banks in any of the most advanced capitalist countries have achieved a "personal union" of industrial and banking capital, and have concentrated in their hands the control of billions upon billions, which form the greatest part of the capital and revenue of an entire country. A financial oligarchy, creating a close network of ties of dependence upon all the economic and political institutions of contemporary bourgeois society without exception —this is the most striking manifestation of this monopoly.

Fourth, monopoly arose out of colonial policy. To the numerous "old" motives of colonial policy finance capital has added the struggle for sources of raw materials, for the export of capital, for "spheres of influence," *i.e.*, spheres of good business, concessions, monopolist profits, and so on; in fine, for economic territory in general. When the colonies of the European powers in Africa comprised only one-tenth of that territory, as was still the case in 1876, colonial policy was able to develop in a non-monopolist manner, like "freebooters" taking land, so to speak. But when nine-tenths of Africa had been seized (by 1900); when the whole world had been divided up, there was inevitably ushered in a period of monopolist possession of colonies, and, consequently, of particularly intense struggle for the partition and for the re-partition of the world....

Monopolies, oligarchy, striving for domination instead of striving for liberty, exploitation of an increasing number of small or weak nations by an extremely small group of the richest or most powerful nations—all these have given birth to those distinctive characteristics of imperialism which compel us to define it as parasitic or decaying capitalism. More and more prominently there appears, as one of the tendencies of imperialism, the creation of the "rentier-state," the user state, whose bourgeoisie lives more and more on capital exports and by "clipping coupons." It would be a mistake to believe that this tendency to decay precludes a rapid growth of capitalism. It does not; in the epoch of imperialism, now one, now another of these tendencies is displayed, to greater or less degree by certain branches of industry, by certain strata of the bourgeoisie, and by individual countries. As a whole, capitalism is growing far more rapidly than before, but not only is this growth becoming more and more uneven, but also this unevenness is showing itself in particular in the decay of the countries which are richest in capital (such as England)....

From all that has been said above on the economic essence of imperialism, it follows that it must be characterised as capitalism in transition, or, more precisely, as dying capitalism....

In 1961 MARK BLAUG (1927–   ), a young Dutch-born economist teaching at Yale University, re-examined various economic theories of imperialism and arrived at conclusions similar to those of an historian, D. K. Fieldhouse. Blaug addressed himself directly to both the factual base and the theoretical structure upon which Lenin had built his thesis, and he found both deficient. The selection below is drawn from Blaug's article; Fieldhouse's analysis follows. Between them they offer a sweeping rebuttal to the economic interpretation put forward by Hobson and Lenin and do so within the framework of the very economic structure Hobson and Lenin used.*

Lenin and Economic Imperialism Reconsidered

Endlessly debated, frequently attacked, still controversial, the theory of economic imperialism is currently enjoying a new lease on life in the underdeveloped countries. When Premier Khrushchev tells an Indian audience that capitalist countries will never extend genuine aid to backward nations "because it would deprive them of their own profits and markets for their goods," he is thinking of Marx and Lenin, not of the record of American foreign aid. But his words find a quick response with most of the nationalist leaders of the newly created countries, providing further evidence of the amazing vitality of the Marxist doctrine of imperialism. In the decades before the First World War it played an important role in socialist debates over the impending breakdown of capitalism; in the 1920's it served to explain the origin and nature of the First World War; in the 1930's it was linked up with the popular view of how Fascism arose in certain Central European countries; and now, since the Second World War, it has turned up in a new guise to discredit Western aid and assistance to the underdeveloped nations.

And yet when examined at all closely, the theory of economic imperialism seems to rest upon slippery grounds; indeed, its proponents have hardly bothered to present a theoretical argument. They have relied for the most part upon familiar underconsumptionist fallacies or simply upon selected descriptions of imperialist policy. No doubt, the history

* From Mark Blaug, "Economic Imperialism Revisited," *Yale Review,* L (March 1961).

of colonialism does not make edifying reading: the story of the imposition of foreign rule never does. But this is not what is at issue. Economic imperialism is a foreign policy that seeks political and economic control over backward areas to guarantee an outlet for idle savings and surplus manufactured goods in exchange for strategic raw materials. Marxist theory supposes that a closed capitalist economy—an economy having no trading relations with other countries—must suffer from chronic insufficiency of effective demand, from basic imbalance that can only be corrected by the opening of foreign markets. Imperialism, the direct or indirect exploitation of backward areas, is therefore an inherent feature of mature capitalism. It would follow that one cannot seriously expect the West to work actively for the raising of living standards in the poor countries of Asia and Africa: the all-round industrialization of these areas would simply spell the doom of capitalism.

This is the thesis I want to examine. Can a closed capitalist economy in principle expand indefinitely on its own resources? If so, the elimination of imperialism would not mean the end of the capitalist system. But if the Marxist arguments stands up, only a socialist society can break away from the imperialist pattern. The question is not whether, say, British rule in Africa was ruinous or beneficent, but whether the Dark Continent was plundered to sustain capitalism in England. Not whether the United States did or did not practice dollar diplomacy in Latin America with the aid of the Marines, but whether a free enterprise economy can help to raise incomes in the Caribbean or Southeast Asia without committing economic suicide. The brute facts marshalled by Lenin and his disciples are all too frequently beyond dispute, but my concern is with the inferences they have drawn from them.

Let us for a moment consider the doctrinal roots of the argument. Lenin's *Imperialism* is thoroughly permeated by Marx's vision of capitalism, subject to chronic underconsumption because wages are slow to rise, if they rise at all, and because investment opportunities dry up as the rate of profit declines. Marx himself talked of colonies as a thing of the past—in his day Britain was said to have acquired her colonies "in a fit of absence of mind"—and abstracted from foreign trade in his central analysis. He believed that on the whole labor was not a beneficiary of economic progress but he refused to be committed to any definite opinion. Even the basic notion that the rate of profit on capital tends to fall through time he only demonstrated by the seemingly plausible but arbitrary assertion that profits per man can never rise as fast as capital per man. Still, Marx, and for that matter John Stuart Mill, did argue that the export of capital, by draining off excess savings, counteracts the decline of the rate of profit in a country. It was not difficult to stretch this into the proposition that the inability to profitably dispose of goods and capital at home leads inevitably to imperialist ventures. The entire theory of economic imperialism was ready made for Lenin by the German followers of Marx and he took it over without further examination, neatly combining in his emphasis upon foreign investment the high-profit pull of backward areas with the low-profit push of late-stage capitalism. . . .

. . . Surely, the prospect of super profits in the poorer countries will induce an outflow of capital from the richer nations? The yield of capital is necessarily higher in backward areas because capital is scarce there and labor is artificially cheap. This kind of argument had considerable a priori appeal in days when foreign investment was a significant fraction of total investment, but it fails to explain . . . why foreign investment took the pattern it did and why the flow of funds to the backward areas was so limited even in the nineteenth century. Nor can it account for the common observation that domestic savings in underdeveloped countries are often hoarded or exported to the advanced capitalist world; if the rate of return is really as high as it is claimed, what prevents local capitalists from emerging?

Contrary to popular belief, however, the yield of capital is generally higher in a capital-rich economy than in an underdeveloped country, because capital in the advanced country is invested in a complementary fashion in basic industry, transport, and power. The potential high yield in capital-poor areas cannot be exploited in the absence of social overhead facilities, such as roads, railways, harbors, docks, dams, power plants, and schools. It rarely pays the individual to invest in these lines since he himself cannot reap their social benefits—this is precisely the argument nowadays for public investment in the underdeveloped countries. Backward countries are generally *not* attractive outlets for private capital. Lenin made his case by simply assuming that social overhead capital, what he called "the elementary conditions for industrial development," was already in existence in the backward areas. But when this was the case, as in Canada and Argentina, the areas did not long remain underdeveloped.

Other things being equal, investors prefer to place their capital at home rather than abroad. The fact that capital was nevertheless exported does indicate that foreign investment offered higher rates of return than domestic investment. But taking into account the risk of inadequate information and the possibility of default, the differential yield was usually more modest than might be expected. Super profits and huge windfalls did occur but losses were not uncommon and on the average it is doubtful whether profits on overseas investment in the nineteenth century exceeded earnings at home by more than one or two percent. . . .

. . . But weak in theory, Lenin's book has nevertheless been praised as giving a succinct review of the facts. The presentation of the record, however, is if anything more suspect than Lenin's theoretical arguments and has given rise to a total misconception of the typical pattern of foreign investment in the heyday of imperialism. . . . The picture of foreign investment which Lenin projects in his book is that of capital exported to low-income staple-producing areas under the direct political control of the major powers concentrating almost exclusively upon the extractive industries, and earning enormous rates of return for a narrow class of investors at home; an accompanying feature is the deliberate dumping of excess supplies upon restricted colonial markets. It is not too much to say that the whole of this is an elegant fiction. Lenin granted, for example, that the bulk of French capital held abroad was invested in Russia, not in the French colonies, while German capital was mostly invested outside her own negligible holdings in Africa. But he insisted that "the principal sphere of investment of British capital is the British colonies," while in fact over half of Britain's foreign assets in the decades before 1914 were held outside the Empire. Even within the Empire, Canada, Australia, and New Zealand—hardly outstanding examples of the ruinous effect of imperialism—accounted for one-half of British investment, and more was invested in Australia and New Zealand alone than in India and the whole of Africa. Outside the Empire the United States and Argentina took the lion's share of British capital. Instead of capital flowing to densely populated China or India, where capital was scarce and labor cheap, two-thirds of Britain's overseas investment in the years 1870-1914 went to the so-called regions of recent settlement, stimulated and complemented by the migration of something like 60 million people. The unique element of capital movements in the classic era of imperialism was just this: capital and labor flowed together from the Old World to the New, a striking fact completely ignored in the Marxist literature. And instead of the backward areas with its "teeming millions" providing the dumping ground for surplus goods, the greater part of British manufactured exports likewise flowed to the regions of recent settlement in the wake of capital and labor....

The fact that very little capital went to the densely populated countries and that most of it was put into fixed-interest bearing government bonds or securities directly guaranteed by some branch of government is surprising only to those held in the grip of the Leninist conception of foreign capital ruthlessly exploiting native labor. Even today, 30 percent of American total direct investment abroad, 37 percent of the foreign branches of American firms, and 50 percent of all American foreign investment in manufacturing is located in Canada, the country with the second highest per capita income in the world.... What is even more striking is that rates of return on foreign investment in the Persian Gulf are as high as 20 percent in contrast to 11 percent in Latin America and 8 percent in Canada; yet the Persian Gulf attracts less than one-tenth of American foreign investment and the rate of increase of foreign investment in the postwar years has been higher in Canada than in the oil-soaked regions of the Middle East. The preference of American investors for relatively developed and culturally familiar economies is a fact difficult to fit into the Leninist theory. And yet it is clear that nonpecuniary motives have always loomed large in determining the flow of international capital....

When the Second World War drew to a close Great Britain was quick to realize that her former colonies could no longer be retained and was generous in granting independence. Even Malaya, with its immense dollar-earning capacity, was given up. Holland and France, on the other hand, refused to surrender their colonies until forced to do so at gun-point. But in the Suez incident and the Cyprus War Britain denied her own claim that colonial rule is justifiable only in so far as it trains a people for self-government. America fulfilled her democratic promises to the Philippines but in Guatemala and Guam took upon herself the mantle of imperialism. The inconsistency of behavior in each case suggests the dominance of political over economic considerations....

One of the most thorough and thoughtful analyses of the Hobson and Lenin interpretations of imperialism yet undertaken was offered in 1961 by a young British historian, D. K. FIELDHOUSE (1925–), Beit Lecturer in the History of the Commonwealth and attached to the Institute of Commonwealth Studies, Oxford. Basing his work on a careful reading of several recent investigations of imperialism, as well as on a reappraisal of Hobson in particular, Fieldhouse raises a number of important questions about the supposed relationship between an exclusively economic interpretation and nineteenth-century imperial development. In doing so, he sets the stage for a consideration of noneconomic causes of imperialism.*

Hobson and Economic Imperialism Reconsidered

It is now nearly sixty years since J. A. Hobson published *Imperialism: a Study,* and thereby gave the word the connotation it still generally carries. His conception of the nature of "imperialism"[1] has, indeed, been almost universally accepted and, partly through the expository literature it has generated, may be said to have exercised a significant historical influence. Yet, for all its success, Hobson's argument has always been extremely vulnerable to criticism: and it is therefore surprising that those historians and economists who have argued effectively that his analysis is basically unsound should have received so little attention....

Hobson's own claim to importance and originality lies simply in his having induced British, and subsequently world, opinion to accept his own special definition of the word imperialism. Professor Koebner[2] has already examined the various meanings given to the word before 1902. He has suggested that, as used in England, it had two general connotations

[1] When used in Hobson's sense, the word will here be printed in inverted commas.

[2] Richard Koebner, 1885–1960, a German-born historian who taught at the University of Berlin and the Hebrew University of Jerusalem, died shortly before the appearance of the first of his two projected volumes on *Empire* (New York, 1961). Here Mr. Fieldhouse is referring to Koebner's "The Concept of Economic Imperialism," *Economic History Review,* 2d ser., II, no. 1 (1949), 1–29—Ed.

* From D. K. Fieldhouse, " 'Imperialism': An Historiographical Revision," *Economic History Review,* 2d ser., XIV (December 1961), 187–209. By permission of the author and the *Economic History Review.* Deletions made by permission of the author.

in the 1890's, both of which were morally neutral. In one sense, it was being used of those who wished to prevent the existing British settlement colonies from seceding and becoming independent states, and was therefore a conservative factor. In another, and increasingly common, sense, it was being used to indicate an expansionist and "forward" attitude towards problems connected with the future control of the "uncivilized" parts of the world, such as Africa, the Middle East and the Pacific. Salisbury[3] was, in this sense, regarded as an imperialist in accepting the need for Britain to share in the partition of East Africa. Gladstone, in opposing the acquisition of Uganda, was emphatically anti-imperialist, even though he had acquiesced in the need to gain some control over Egypt in 1882. In the eyes of the anti-imperialists the sin of expansionism lay in the waste of money it entailed on armaments, in the cost of colonial governments, and in the danger of international conflicts over intrinsically unimportant territories which it would be wiser to leave alone. As a rule no worse motive was attributed to the imperialists than "jingoism" or excessive concern with Britain's position as a great power.

But, between 1896 and 1902, imperialism, as a word, began to lose its innocence. Koebner has shown that events in South Africa, and particularly the Jameson Raid, gave rise to a suspicion that, here at least, the expansive urge was motivated by something other than a concern for national greatness, by what Harcourt[4] called "stock-jobbing imperialism"—based on the interests of financiers. This was, of course, a special case; and a distinction remained between an honest, even if misguided, imperialism, and the debased variety to be seen on the Rand. Yet the idea now gained ground that South Africa might not, after all, be a special case, but might exhibit in an extreme form a factor inherent in all expansionism. . . .

Hobson's *Imperialism* therefore came out at a time when British public opinion, disillusioned by the Boer war, was already profoundly suspicious about the motives behind recent imperial expansion. It was, in fact, a pamphlet for the times, rather than a serious study of the subject; and, like all pamphlets that achieve influence, it owed much of its success to the fact that it expressed a current idea with peculiar clarity, force and conviction. . . . Yet, paradoxically, Hobson was not primarily concerned with imperial problems: and *Imperialism* can only be properly understood on the basis that his interest, then and throughout his life, was with the social and economic problems of Britain. In a sense, this book was primarily a vehicle for publicizing the theory of "underconsumption," which he regarded as his main intellectual achievement, and which he expressed more fully in *The Evolution of Modern Capitalism,* and other works. . . .

. . . Thus "imperialism," in the special sense used by Hobson, is an external symptom of a social malady in the metropolitan countries. Without . . . domestic pressure for investment overseas, there would be no effective impulse towards the acquisition of new colonies. Conversely, without colonies, capital would

[3] Lord Salisbury was British prime minister on three occasions: 1885–1886, 1886–1892, and 1895–1902. During much of this time he acted as his own foreign secretary as well—Ed.

[4] Sir William V. Harcourt, 1827–1904, barrister, professor of international law at Cambridge, leader of the Liberal party 1896–1898, was a member of the House of Commons' select committee that censured Cecil Rhodes because of the Jameson Raid—Ed.

lack an outlet, and domestic rates of interest would sink....

[S]ome comment must be made on the logical value of the argument [Hobson] uses to demonstrate the historical truth of this hypothesis. Does he, in fact, supply any evidence to support the claim that colonies were the product of a demand either for new investment opportunities, or for security for existing investments? He begins with a straightforward account of the expansion of the European empires since 1870, printing a list of territories acquired by Britain, which Lenin ... reproduced. Then he demonstrates that the expansion of the British empire had been of little apparent value to British trade; that trade with these recent acquisitions was the least valuable part of intra-imperial trade; and that British trade with all colonies was declining in relation to trade with the rest of the world.[5] Clearly, then, "imperialism" was not good for trade. Nor was it good for emigration (which, in any case, he thought unnecessary), since these new tropical colonies were quite unsuited to white settlement. And his conclusion was that

The Imperialism of the last six decades is clearly condemned as a business policy, in that at enormous expense it has procured a small, bad, unsafe increase of markets, and has jeopardised the entire wealth of the nation in arousing the strong resentment of other nations....

How then can a motive be found for this imperial expansion? The motive is to be seen if, alongside the list of territorial acquisitions, is placed a table showing the increase of British overseas investments in the same period. It then becomes obvious that, during the period in which British possessions had increased by 4,754 m. square miles and by a population of 88 millions, British overseas investments had also increased enormously—from £144 m. to £1698 m. between 1862 and 1893 alone. Could there be any doubt that the two sets of figures were intimately connected as cause and effect? Hobson had no doubts about it: "It is not too much to say that the modern foreign policy of Great Britain has been primarily a struggle for profitable markets of investment."

But it is immediately apparent that Hobson had in no sense proved that there was any connexion between the investments made overseas and the territory acquired contemporaneously. His table of investments makes no differentiation between the areas in which investment had taken place, beyond such classifications as "Foreign," "Colonial," "U.S.A." and "Various," and, in fact, he assumes quite arbitrarily that the new colonies had attracted a high proportion of the investment called "Foreign" (i.e. before they were annexed) or "Colonial" (subsequent to annexation). This ... is a basic fault of his theory of "imperialism." Indeed, to put the case bluntly, Hobson performed an intellectual conjuring trick. Convinced of the essential truth of his economic theory, he deceived the eye by the speed of his hand, creating the illusion that, of the two sets of statistics he held up, one was the cause of the other....

[Two] additional points in his main argument must be mentioned because

[5] Hobson based this conclusion on figures taken from Cd. 1761, p. 407.... These were inaccurate. A.K. Cairncross (*Home and Foreign Investment 1870–1913* [Cambridge University Press, 1953], p. 189), shows that British exports to the empire increased from 24 per cent to 33.6 per cent of total British trade between 1870–2 and 1890–2, and imports from 21.9 per cent to 22.9 per cent in the same period. Both percentages continued to increase to 1910–12. But Hobson was right in saying that the new colonies contributed little to the increased volume of intra-imperial trade.

they were intrinsic to his definition of the origins and nature of "imperialist" expansion.

The first of these concerns the relationship between the financial interest and other "imperialists," and is therefore crucial to his theory. He was aware that, contrary to his argument, the obvious driving force of British expansion since 1870 appeared to lie in the explorers, missionaries, engineers, patriotic pressure groups, and empire-minded politicians, all of whom had evident influence, and had demonstrable interests, other than those of investment, in territorial acquisitions. And he was equally aware that if the impulse to expansion could be satisfactorily explained in the old-fashioned terms of their idealism, their ambition, or their concern with the status of Britain as a world power, rather than in terms of the self-interest of the capitalist, his own central thesis would collapse. It was therefore necessary that these men . . . should be shown to be mere puppets—the tools of "imperialism" rather than its authors. Hobson did this by falling back on what may be called the "faceless men" gambit:

> Finance manipulates the patriotic forces which politicians, soldiers, philanthropists, and traders generate; the enthusiasm for expansion which issues from these sources, though strong and genuine, is irregular and blind; the financial interest has those qualities of concentration and clear-sighted calculation which are needed to set Imperialism to work. An ambitious statesman, a frontier soldier, an overzealous missionary, a pushing trader, may suggest or even initiate a step of imperial expansion, may assist in educating patriotic public opinion to the urgent need of some fresh advance, but the final determination rests with the financial power.

In this ingenious way Hobson inverted the apparent relationship between the obvious "imperialists" and the investor. Instead of the financier being induced to invest in new possessions, with more or less enthusiasm, once political control had been imposed for other reasons, he becomes the essential influence in the take-over itself. . . . Thus, "imperialism" can never be interpreted as the spontaneous expression of the idealism, the chauvinism or the mere energy of a nation. In its practical form it is the expression of the special interests of the financier behind the scenes, who decides whether it is worth his while to allow a dream to become a reality, and who alone will reap the benefits. . . .

The other essential point in the theory of "imperialism" is the suggestion that the possession of colonies by individual capitalist states results automatically in the exploitation of the indigenous peoples of Africa and Asia. In his long chapter "Imperialism and the Lower Races," . . . Hobson argued that exploitation, whether by appropriation of land, or by the use of cheap labour —forced or nominally free—in mines, farms and factories, had been a general feature of the colonies of all the European powers. Hobson, in the British humanitarian tradition, thought such exploitation to be both wrong and inexpedient. Economic development was good for undeveloped colonies and for the world as a whole. The danger lay in allowing the financiers to use the political power of the imperial authority for their own purposes; and the solution was for international control of colonies —the germ of the later mandate concept —and patience in allowing normal economic forces to give the natives an inducement to work freely in European enterprises. Sensible as his general attitude was, it is clear that Hobson had thus included in "imperialism" the suggestion that countries possessing colonies were almost certain to exploit them in their own interests; and this argument was to become a staple of later critics of "colonialism".

. . . Yet, . . . it is clear that it was Lenin, writing in 1916, rather than Hobson himself, who gave "imperialism" its dogmatic coherence and much of its eventual influence. It is therefore necessary to consider briefly the extent to which Lenin modified Hobson's ideas.

The greatest difference lies in the first and most important part of the argument; that is, in the nature of the internal pressure in the capitalist countries which forces them to expand their colonial possessions. Hobson had explained this pressure in terms of "under-consumption": but Lenin naturally had a more orthodox theory to hand. Capitalism as a system was approaching the apocalypse Marx had foretold. Competitive capitalism had, in the late nineteenth century, been replaced by "monopoly capitalism," with its characteristic agencies, the cartels, trusts and tariffs. It was no longer dynamic, but anxious only to maintain its profit margins by more intensive exploitation of limited and protected markets. Moreover, the "finance-capitalists"—the banks and trusts—who now largely controlled capital itself, found that, under monopoly conditions, it was more profitable to employ surplus capital abroad than in domestic industry. At home, it could only increase production, lower prices, and raise wages. Abroad it could give a high interest return without any of these consequences. But, to gain the highest return from overseas investment it was desirable to have some political control over the territory in which the investment was made. This might be in the limited form of a "semi-colony," such as the Argentine. But only in the colony proper could really comprehensive economic and political controls be imposed which would give investments their highest return. The result had been the competition between the great powers to acquire new colonies after 1870, which would continue until the whole uncivilized world had come under imperial rule. Then would follow the inter-imperial wars for the redivision of the empires, leading to proletarian revolutions in the "imperialist" states, the creation of "socialist" states, and so, automatically, to the end of "imperialism."

How much, then, does Lenin's explanation of the force behind "imperialism" differ from that of Hobson? Fundamentally, only in this: that, whereas Hobson used his theory as evidence that social-democratic reform at home was necessary and possible to eliminate the evil of "under-consumption" and therefore make "imperialism" unnecessary, Lenin made "imperialism" the definition of an inherent and unavoidable stage in the growth of capitalist society which could not be "reformed." Hobson was a doctor prescribing a remedy, Lenin a prophet forecasting catastrophe.[6]. . .

. . . The central feature of the theory of "imperialism," by which it must stand or fall, is the assertion that the empires built up after 1870 were not an option but a necessity for the economically advanced states of Europe and America: that these capitalist societies, because of their surplus of domestically produced capital, were forced to export capital to the under-developed regions of the world: and that it was only this investment—propective or existing—that sup-

[6] There are, of course, many other differences which cannot be considered here, e.g. Hobson ignored "semi-colonies," and thought of "finance" as operating in an essentially free-trade environment.

plied a motive for the acquisition of new colonies.

Faced with this theory, the historian who does not take its truth for granted is likely to be sceptical on at least three main grounds. First, his instinct is to distrust all-embracing historical formulas which, like the concept of "the rise of the middle class," seek to explain complex developments in terms of a single dominant influence. Again, he is likely to suspect an argument that isolates the imperial expansion of the period after 1870 from all earlier imperial developments if only because he is aware of so many elements of continuity in the history of overseas empires over the past few centuries. But, above all, he must be aware that the theory simply does not appear to fit the facts of the post-1870 period as he knows them. Looking, for example, at Hobson's list of territories acquired by Britain after 1870, it seems, at first sight at least, difficult to believe that any considerable part of them were annexed either because British capitalists had already invested much of their surplus capital there, or because they regarded them as fields for essential future investment. In some cases, perhaps, it seems that a *prima facie* case could be made out on these lines—for Egypt, the Transvaal and Rhodesia, to take Hobson's three main examples. But, even in these, further consideration must arouse doubts. Surely the strategic importance of the Suez Canal was as good a reason for controlling Egypt in 1882 as the preservation of the interests of the bond holders in the Canal Company. Was it really necessary, on purely economic grounds, to annex the Transvaal in 1899 when the British mine-owners were making vast fortunes under Kruger's government, and had shown themselves so divided over the question of the Jameson Raid and the independence of the Republic? Again, granted that Rhodes and the British South Africa Company had excellent economic reasons for wanting British control over Rhodesia, was their anxiety really due to the pressure of British funds waiting for investment opportunity?

Doubts such as these concerning even the key examples chosen by Hobson inevitably stimulate further examination of his list: and this makes it clear that not even a *prima facie* case could be made out for most of the territories he includes. To take a random selection, it would surely be ludicrous to suggest that Fiji, British New Guinea or Upper Burma were annexed in order to protect large British investments, or even as a field for subsequent investment. In each case secular explanations seem fully to account for their annexation: the chaotic condition of a mixed society in the Pacific, the fears of Australia for her military security, and the frontier problems of India. And even where, as in Malaya, large capital investment did take place after annexation, the time factor must be considered. Were the British investor and the government really so alert to the possible future need for fields for investment? Or did annexation in fact take place for quite other reasons, being followed by investment when new conditions and new possibilities arose which were then totally unforeseen?

Yet, obvious though the weakness of the theory of "imperialism" may seem when applied in specific cases, it is also clear that it would be extremely difficult to invalidate Hobson's model by a process of piecemeal examination. For the adherents of this, as of most comprehensive formulas, could counter . . . by asserting that an analytical explanation of the phenomenon merely supplied "an unaccountable jumble of facts and dates..." or,... by calling all annexations that do not fit demonstrably into the pattern "protective and anticipatory," or based on "considerations of a strategic nature." That is, they could fight an indefinite rearguard action.... Moreover, if the theory is false, it should be possible to demonstrate that its premises are false also. And, since the essential premise of "imperialism" is the belief that the drive to acquire colonies after 1870 was the direct and necessary result of the need of the capitalists to export capital, this proposition demands careful examination.

It has been seen that this theory of surplus capital being forced out into the undeveloped world was expressed differently by Hobson and Lenin, and it will be convenient to consider Lenin's theory first. This was, it will be remembered, that the centrifugal force in the capitalist countries was the interest of the monopolistic "finance-capitalists" who stood only to lose by investment at home.

In this the fallacy is immediately obvious. If it was true of any country, it was not true of Britain; for no one could maintain that British capital was then controlled by a few trusts or even cartels. These, of course, did exist in Britain, such as the Salt Union of 1888, the United Alkali Company of 1897, and others in textiles, shipping and steel. But, whatever the desires of their founders, they were in fact small, tentative and generally unsuccessful. British capital, whatever its tendencies, was still "competitive" on Lenin's definition: and he in fact admitted that in Britain "monopoly" must be taken to mean the reduction of the competing enterprises to "a couple of dozen or so." This is hardly a satisfactory explanation of the need to export capital on a vast scale; so, presumably, Britain must have other reasons both for this and for territorial annexation. But, for different reasons, other countries also escape from the formula. Germany was Lenin's main example of the country dominated by trusts: but, as Professor Hancock has pointed out,[7] the age of German cartels came only after about 1900, while the main German grab for colonies had taken place during the previous twenty years. And America, which certainly had vast industrial and financial combinations, proved, in spite of [Theodore] Roosevelt's attempt to create an expansionist movement, to be the least "imperialist" of all the capitalist states. It would therefore seem reasonable to conclude that Lenin's narrow explanation for the export of capital and the concurrent extension of European political control overseas is unacceptable.

Yet, whatever reasons are assigned to it, the fact of vast capital exports from the advanced countries in the period after 1870 remains. Sir G[eorge] Paish, in his much quoted article,[8] estimated that British overseas investment had increased between 1871 and 1911 from £785 m. to £3500 m., with a possible margin of error of 10 per cent either way. These figures are necessarily highly speculative; but there is no question that they were extremely large. And it is quite possible, even while rejecting Lenin's doctrinaire explanation, to see in the fact of this investment support for Hobson's theory that the urge to invest was the main cause of imperial

7 W.K. Hancock, *The Wealth of Colonies* (Cambridge, 1950), pp. 11–12.

8 "Great Britain's Capital Investments in Individual Colonial and Foreign Countries," *Journal of the Royal Statistical Society*, LXXIV (January 1911), 167–200. John Maynard Keynes was present in the audience and criticized Paish's paper. (Expanded note—Ed.)

expansion. Hence, the important questions must be faced. Was there in fact a vast reservoir of capital, generated (for example) in Britain, which was available for overseas investment? Why was it invested abroad rather than at home? And was it in fact invested in those areas which were annexed as colonies after 1871?

The publication in 1953 of Professor A. K. Cairncross's *Home and Foreign Investment 1870–1913* has made it possible to approach these questions from a new and non-doctrinaire angle. The key to his interpretation lay in his rejection of Hobson's naive model of the British capitalist, embarrassed by an excess of capital, which could not be invested at home because of the "underconsumption" factor, sending it abroad into undeveloped tropical territories where it would produce a high rate of interest. Instead, it is necessary to see that capital exports were not divorced from the economy of Great Britain but were in fact a necessary concomitant of the pattern of British trade and development. It can be shown that in fact the great majority of this capital went to the "new" countries—to the United States, Canada, [the] Argentine, Australasia and South Africa in particular—who were producing the primary materials that the British economy needed, and who had to have capital to expand their production for British consumption. To invest in these countries was therefore, in one sense, to invest in a primary sector of the British economy itself. And the return to Britain was not entirely, or even primarily, in a tribute of money, but in cheap and plentiful raw materials and food.

Moreover, far from weakening the British economy and reducing the living standards of the working class as both Hobson and Lenin thought they did, these capital exports were essential to both. Indeed, Cairncross argues convincingly that, by creating a demand for British products, these investments simultaneously kept up the level of profits at home, kept down the level of unemployment, and maintained wage levels. And, as the rate of overseas investment seems to have been greatest when the terms of trade were against Britain—the 1880's being an exceptional period when special factors in the United States offset the general tendency—Cairncross concludes that "it was foreign investment that pulled Britain out of most depressions before 1914."

Seen, therefore, from the point of view of Britain's part in the world economy, rather than in purely domestic terms, capital exports no longer seem to have been forced out of the British economy by the selfish interests of the capitalists to maintain artificially high interest rates, and become, as Professor Nurkse[9] has described them, "a means whereby a vigorous process of economic growth came to be transmitted from the centre to the outlying areas of the world." That is to say that the force behind the export of capital was the pull exerted by urgent need for capital in the newly-developing countries, who, because of their higher potential productivity and because markets were available for their exports, could afford to pay higher rates of interest than were obtainable in Britain. Yet, important though it was in explaining why the British and European investor chose to send his capital abroad, this differential in rates of interest should not be overestimated. For the years 1905–9

[9] Ragnar Nurkse (1907–1959), an Estonian-born economist who taught at Columbia University, is best known for his *Problems of Capital Formation in Underdeveloped Countries* (5th ed.; New York, 1953). The quotation here comes from his *Patterns of Trade and Development* (Stockholm, 1959), p. 14. (Expanded note—Ed.)

Lehfeldt[10] calculated the average interest on home, colonial and overseas investments to be 3.61 per cent, 3.94 per cent and 4.97 per cent respectively. But even this to some extent obscures the real facts of the situation. The interest on British consols might be only 2.88 per cent: but rates of over 5 per cent were available on other British stocks, such as railway debentures and industrials. Equally, in railway loans, which were the most popular type of British overseas investment in the years before 1914, the interest rates varied from a mere 3.87 per cent on India railways to 4.7 per cent in foreign railways. In fact it can be said that the British investor did not choose to invest abroad simply to get high interest rates, but, by and large, to get a slightly higher rate than on an equivalent type of stock at home. Above all, if he chose to invest in a British colony, it was not because he expected higher interest, but because he wanted greater security than he would get in an equivalent foreign investment. If he wanted a "risk" investment—diamonds, copper, gold, nitrates, etc.—he went for it wherever the enterprise happened to be situated. But, in proportion to the whole, investments of this type were very small in 1911.

But, for the present argument, the third and most important fact that emerges from the work of Paish, Cairncross and Nurkse is that Hobson was entirely wrong in assuming that any large proportion of British overseas investment went to those undeveloped parts of Africa and Asia which were annexed during the "imperialist" grab after 1870. As Professor Nurkse has remarked of Hobson:

> Had he tried to do what he did for trade, that is, to show the geographical distribution of overseas investment, he would have found that British capital tended to bypass the primitive tropical economies and flowed mainly to the regions of recent settlement outside as well as inside the British Empire.[11]

And the figures published by Paish in 1911 demonstrate this conclusively. The bulk of British investment then lay in the United States, £688 m., South America, £587 m., Canada, £372 m., Australasia, £380 m., India and Ceylon, £365 m., and South Africa, £351 m. By contrast, West Africa had received only £29 m., the Straits and Malay States, £22 m., and the remaining British possessions, £33 m. These last were, of course, by no means negligible amounts, and indicate clearly that in some at least of the tropical dependencies which had been recently acquired, British finance was finding scope for profit and investment. But this does not make Hobson's thesis any more valid. The sums invested in these tropical areas, whether newly annexed or not, were quite marginal to the total overseas investment, and continued to be relatively very small in the years immediately before 1911. Hence, to maintain that Britain had found it necessary to acquire these territories because of an urgent need for new fields for investment is simply unrealistic: and, with the rejection of this hypothesis, so ingeniously conjured up by Hobson, the whole basis of his theory that "imperialism" was the product of economic necessity collapses.

But to suggest that Hobson and Lenin were mistaken in thinking that the need to export capital from Europe after 1870 was so intense that it made the colonization of most of Africa and the Pacific necessary as fields for investment is merely to throw the question open again. The essential problem remains: on what other grounds is it possible to explain this sudden expansion of European pos-

[10] R. A. Lehfeldt, British economist and statistician, quoted in Cairncross, p. 227. (Expanded note—Ed.)

[11] Nurkse, p. 19.

sessions, whose motive force is called imperialism? . . .

Looking broadly over the four centuries since the early Portuguese discoveries, it may be said that, although European motives for acquiring colonies were extremely complex, they fell into two general categories. First was the specifically economic motive, whose aim was to create a lucrative trade for the metropolitan country. Its typical expression was the trading base or factory, secured by some form of agreement with the local ruler: but, where no commodities already existed for trade, it could result in territorial possessions, like the sugar islands of the Caribbean, or the spice islands of the East; the fur-producing parts of North America, and the silver mines of Peru. The export of capital played no significant part in this economic activity, for Europe had little surplus capital before the nineteenth century, and investment was restricted to the immediate needs of trade itself, of the mines, sugar estates, etc.

By contrast, it is clear that from the earliest days of European expansion the margin between economic and other motives was small, and that many colonies were rather the product of political and military rivalries than of the desire for profit. The mercantile practices followed by all European states were as much concerned with national power as with economic advantage, and tended, as Adam Smith pointed out, to subordinate opulence to the needs of security. Indeed, by the eighteenth century, imperial policies had come to be largely a reflection of European power politics: and the struggle for territorial supremacy in America, India and the strategic bases on the route to the East were the outcome of political rather than of strictly economic competition. Britain's decision to retain Canada rather than Guadaloupe in 1763 may perhaps stand as an example of preference given to a colony offering mainly military security and prestige over one whose value was purely economic.

If, then, a general view of pre-nineteenth century imperial policies shows the complexity of its aims—made still more complicated in the early nineteenth century by the important new element of humanitarianism—it must seem surprising that Hobson should have interpreted post-1870 imperialism in narrowly economic terms, and have ignored the possibility that strictly political impulses may once again have been of major importance. The reason would seem to be that the evolution of imperial practices since about 1815 appeared, at the end of the century, to have constituted a clear break with earlier methods; to have made both the economic and the political criteria of earlier times irrelevant; and thus to have made comparison pointless. With the independence of almost all the American colonies, and the subsequent adoption by Britain—the chief remaining colonial power—of the practices of free trade, the possession of colonies no longer offered any positive economic advantage. The colonial trades were now open to all; bullion-hunting became the function of the individual prospector; and emigration, although it led to new British colonies in Australasia, flowed more naturally into the existing states of the new world. On the political side also, colonies had ceased to play an important part in diplomacy. With the preponderance of Britain as a naval power, and the weakness of most European states, power politics were largely restricted to Britain, France and Russia. As between them competitive aggressiveness was recurrent: but, except briefly in the Pacific, and more frequently in the Near East and on the borders of India, their rivalry did not produce any major competition for new territory. And this seemed to imply that the end of mercantilism had been followed by the end also of political imperialism: which in turn suggested that the renewal of a general international desire for colonies after 1870 must have sprung from some new phenomenon—the unprecedented need to acquire openings for the safe investment of surplus capital.

It is mainly because Hobson's theory of "imperialism" in his own time was based on this theory of discontinuity in nineteenth century history that it must be regarded as fallacious. For there had, in fact, been no break in the continuity of imperial development; merely a short-term variation in the methods used, corresponding with a temporary change in world conditions. In the first place, the extension of the territorial possessions of the three surviving great powers continued intermittently throughout: and the list of British acquisitions between 1840 and 1871 alone bears comparison with those of the following thirty years. On what grounds, in this period of so-called "anti-imperialism," are these to be explained? Obviously no single explanation will serve. Hong Kong stood alone as a trading base with a specifically economic function. Queensland was the result of internal expansion in Australia, British Columbia of rivalry from the United States. But the rest—the Punjab, Sind, Berar, Oudh and Lower Burma on the frontiers of British India; Basutoland, Griqualand and (temporarily) the Transvaal on the Cape frontier; and small areas round existing trading bases in West Africa—stand as evidence that an existing empire will tend always to expand its boundaries. They were not the product of an expansive British policy, but of the need for military security, for administrative efficiency, or for the protection of indigenous peoples on the frontiers of existing colonies. Basically, they demonstrated the fact, familiar in earlier centuries, that colonies which exist in a power vacuum will tend always to expand slowly until they meet with some immovable political or geographical obstacle; and that a metropolitan government can do little more than slow down the speed of movement. For the purpose of the present argument this process may be said to indicate that Hobson needed no new explanation for the bulk of British acquisitions after 1870: for, as has already been pointed out, most of the new colonies on his list differed little in type or situation from those just mentioned—and were indeed mostly the extension of the same colonial frontiers. And, to this extent, late nineteenth century imperialism was merely the continuation of a process which had begun centuries earlier.

At the same time, it must be said that this "contiguous area" theory does not fully cover certain of the new British possessions on Hobson's list. For some of them, like East Africa, were not strictly contiguous to an existing British colony; and others, such as Nigeria or Rhodesia, were clearly annexed too suddenly and on too large a scale to be seen as the product of the domestic needs of Lagos or the Cape. These therefore suggest that some other factor was at work—competition for new colonies on political grounds. . . .

Again, in the sphere of economic policy, the antithesis between different parts of the nineteenth century were greatly exaggerated and misunderstood by Hobson. The rejection of most of the mercantile devices for stimulating European trade had not meant that trade ceased to be a matter of national concern, or that governments ceased to use political means to support their men of business; the contrast with earlier centuries lay mainly in the methods now used. Hobson seemed to think that free trade had ended "economic imperialism" of the mercantile variety simply because political control was no longer regarded as a prerequisite for economic exploitation of an undeveloped area. But, as Messrs. [John] Gallagher and [Ronald] Robinson have pointed out,[12] "formal" control, as in a colony, was not the only way in which "economic imperialism" could operate; indeed, it now had two complementary features. On its specifically economic side it implied, as always, the control of the economic assets of some other country for the advantage of the metropolitan state. And the essential weapons of the European trader or financier were economic—the demand for his goods, his capital or his credit, and the effectiveness of the organization he built up in a country lacking business organization.... By the end of the nineteenth century most of the world had been . . . brought under the economic control of European, and now also United States, business enterprise: their trade was organized and carried by foreign merchants, their revenues mortgaged to the loans they had received. This indeed was "economic imperialism" in its purest form; cosmopolitan in outlook, unconcerned with political frontiers, showing no interest in the creation of "formal" colonies except where, as in China, the formula of the open door proved otherwise unworkable. Only in the absolute volume of its activity, and in the increasing competition between rivals from newly industrialized countries, did the character of "economic imperialism" change before 1914. And, while it remained thus strictly economic and cosmopolitan, the "division of the world among the international trusts," which Lenin prophesied, remained a possibility.

Yet, even in its classical form, "economic imperialism" required political support from governments at home: and, in view of developments after about 1870, it is important to define the nature of the support it received. Essentially the men of business needed only two things which their own enterprise could not supply: a minimum standard of political security at the periphery, and the solution of the quasi-political problems arising out of their relations with foreign rivals by diplomatic action at the centre. The first need was met by the network of treaties made for them with their client countries which secured equality of opportunity and reasonable tariffs, and was backed up, where necessary, by the use of threats and force. In the environment of the free world economy, these were the equivalents of the commercial monopolies of the mercantile period in that they supplied the political basis for successful business enterprise in undeveloped countries.

Second, and parallel with this, went the constant diplomatic work of the foreign offices of Europe in maintaining the balance between their nationals at the circumference. On the common assumption that it was to the general interest that competition should remain fair, that an artificial monopoly was to the advantage of none, and that such problems must not be allowed to harm interna-

12 "The Imperialism of Free Trade," *Economic History Review*, 2d ser., VI (1953), 1–15. This influential article has been critically analyzed by Oliver MacDonagh in "The Anti-Imperialism of Free Trade," *ibid.*, XIV (April 1962), 489–501. (Expanded note—Ed.)

tional relations, diplomacy sought to settle these disputes without taking refuge in unilateral annexation of the area concerned. In this it was generally successful, where the will to succeed existed. . . .

It is now possible to place the imperialism of the period of Hobson's *Study* in its historical context, and to attempt a definition of the extent to which it differed from that of earlier years. The most obvious fact on which his theory was based was that, by contrast with the preceding half-century, vast areas of the world were quickly brought under European control for the first time: and it is now evident that this cannot be explained in terms of either of the two tendencies operating throughout the earlier nineteenth century. Although the break with the past was not as sharp as Hobson seemed to think, it remains true that many British annexations cannot be explained on the "contiguous area" theory: and the new possessions of France, Italy and Germany were quite definitely in a different category. But neither can these facts be explained on Hobson's theory: for, as has been said, the places now to be taken over had hitherto attracted little capital, and did not attract it in any quantity subsequently. Nor, again, can an explanation be found in the more general theory of "economic imperialism," for these places in the Pacific and in Africa for which the nations now competed were of marginal economic importance; and, on the assumptions of the past fifty years, governments might have been expected to reject demands by their nationals for annexation of territories whose administrative costs would be out of all proportion to their economic value to the nation. . . . What, then, was the explanation?

An answer is not, of course, hard to find, and indeed emerges clearly from the vast literature now available. With the exception of the supporters of the "imperialism" thesis, the concensus of opinion is very marked. The new factor in imperialism was . . . essentially a throwback to some of the characteristic attitudes and practices of the eighteenth century. Just as, in the early nineteenth century, the economic interests had demanded effectively that imperial questions should no longer be decided on political grounds, demanding opulence in place of security, so, at the end of the century, the balance was again reversed. The outstanding feature of the new situation was the subordination of economic to political considerations, the preoccupation with national security, military power and prestige.

Again, reasons are not hard to find. The significant fact about the years after 1870 was that Europe became once again an armed camp. The creation of a united Germany, the defeat of Austria and, above all, of France were to dominate European thinking until 1914. Between Germany and France there stood the question of Alsace-Lorraine: and for both the primary consideration was now a system of alliances which would, on the German side, prevent French counterattack, on the French side, make revenge possible. Inevitably the rest of Europe was drawn into the politics of the balance of power between them; and for all statesmen military strength became once again the criterion of national greatness. Inevitably too this situation, with its similarities to the politics of the eighteenth century, brought in its train a return to many of the attitudes of mercantilism. Emigration to foreign states, instead of being regarded as an economic safety valve, became once again a loss of military or manufacturing manpower;

and population statistics became a measure of relative national strength. Protective tariffs came back also, with the primary aim of building up national self-sufficiency and the power to make war.

Under such circumstances it was only to be expected that colonies would be regarded once again as assets in the struggle for power and status: but in fact the attitude of the powers to the imperial question was not at first a simple one. Indeed, it cannot be said that the attitudes characteristic of "the imperialism of free trade" were seriously weakened until the mid-1880's; and until then it seemed possible that the colonial question might be kept clear of European politics. This is not in fact surprising. For most of the men who then ruled Europe retained a realistic appreciation of the potential value to their countries of those parts of the world that were available for annexation. Bismarck in particular recognized that, as sources of raw materials, as fields for emigration or as spheres for trade, the areas available in Africa and the Pacific had little to offer Germany, whatever national advantages those with private interests there might claim. At best they might offer naval bases, a strictly limited trade, and bargaining counters for use in diplomacy. It is improbable that Bismarck ever really changed this opinion: and, while he held off, it was unlikely that any other power would feel strong enough to precipitate a rush for new colonies. . . .

It was, therefore, Bismarck's action in 1884–5, in announcing the formal control by Germany over parts of West and South West Africa, and of New Guinea, that really began the new phase of political imperialism: and it is therefore important to consider his reasons for giving Germany a "colonial policy." . . . In 1884 Bismarck seems to have decided that it was time for him to stop playing the honest broker in the disputes of other powers over their own possessions—such as Egypt and the Congo—and that, on two counts, both essentially diplomatic, Germany should now stake her own claims to colonies. The first was that it was politically desirable to show France that his recent support for Britain on the Egyptian question did not imply a general hostility towards her, since he was now prepared to take action resented by Britain: the second that Britain should be made to see that German support for her in the colonial field must be repaid by closer co-operation in Europe.

In a narrow sense, then, the race for colonies was the product of diplomacy rather than of any more positive force. Germany set the example by claiming exclusive control over areas in which she had an arguable commercial stake, but no more, as a means of adding a new dimension to her international bargaining power, both in respect of what she had already taken, and of what she might claim in the future. Thereafter the process could not be checked; for, under conditions of political tension, the fear of being left out of the partition of the globe overrode all practical considerations. Perhaps Britain was the only country which showed genuine reluctance to take a share; and this was due both to her immense stake in the continuance of the *status quo* for reasons of trade, and to her continued realism in assessing the substantive value of the lands under dispute. And the fact that she too joined in the competition demonstrated how contagious the new political forces were. Indeed, until the end of the century, imperialism may best be seen as the extension into the periphery of the political struggle in Europe. At the centre the balance was so nicely adjusted that no positive action, no major change in the status or territory of either side was possible. Colonies thus became a means out of the impasse; sources of diplomatic strength, prestige-giving accessions of territory, hope for future economic development. New worlds were being brought into existence in the vain hope that they would maintain or redress the balance of the old.

This analysis of the dynamic force of the new imperialism has been stated in purely political terms. What part was played in it by the many non-political interests with a stake in the new colonies: the traders, the investors, the missionaries, and the speculators? For these were the most vociferous exponents of a "forward" policy in most countries: and to men like Hobson it seemed that their influence, if backed by that of the greater interest of the financier, was decisive in causing the politicians to act.

Again the problem is complex. In general terms the answer would seem to be that, while statesmen were very much aware of the pressure groups—conscious of the domestic political advantage of satisfying their demands, and often themselves sympathetic to the case they put up—they were not now, any more than earlier in the century, ready to undertake the burden of new colonies simply on their account. What made it seem as if these interests were now calling the tune was that the choice facing the statesman was no longer between annexation and the continued independence of the area in question: it was now between action and allowing a rival to step in.... Yet if, in the last resort, the decision by Britain or any other country to annex was based on the highest reasons of state, it also true that the very existence of these hitherto embarrassing pressure groups now became a diplomatic asset, since they were the obvious grounds on which valid claims could be made, an approximation to the principle of effective occupation.

Thus the relative importance of the concrete interests and demands of the various pressure groups, as compared with the political criteria of the statesmen, was the reverse of that assigned to them by Hobson. . . . [B]y the time Hobson wrote in 1902, those who supported a "forward" policy were no longer the few diplomatic chess-players, nor even the relatively small pressure groups, but millions of people for whom an empire had become a matter of faith. Indeed, the rise of this imperialist ideology, this belief that colonies were an essential attribute of any great nation, is one of the most astonishing facts of the period. It was, moreover, an international creed, with beliefs that seemed to differ very little from one country to another.... By the end of the century, the "imperial idea," as it has significantly been called, after twenty years of propaganda by such groups of enthusiasts as the German *Kolonverein* and the British Imperial Federation League, had become dominant....

...[B]y [1903–1905] imperialism had been shown to be a delusion. It was already the common experience of all the countries that had taken part in the partition of Africa and the Pacific that, except for the few windfalls, such as gold in West Africa, diamonds in South West Africa, and copper in the Congo and Rhodesia, the new colonies were white elephants: and that only small sectional interests in any country had obtained real benefits from them. Whether German, French, British or Italian, their trade was minute (German trade with her colonies was only ½ per cent of her external trade); their attraction for investors, except in mines, etc., was negligible; they were unsuitable for large-scale emigration, and any economic development that had taken place was usually the result of determined efforts by the European state concerned to create an artificial asset. Moreover, in most cases, the cost of administration was a dead weight on the imperial power. By 1900 all these facts were apparent and undeniable. They were constantly pressed by opponents of colonial expansion in each country; and Hobson's book consisted primarily of an exposition of these defects. Yet public opinion was increasingly oblivious to such facts: the possession of colonies had become a sacred cow, a psychological necessity. While the financiers continued to invest their money, as they had done in the previous fifty years, in economically sound projects, such as the Baghdad railway, in the non-tropical settlement colonies and independent countries, and in places like India—remaining true to the criteria of true "economic imperialism"—the politicians, pressed on now by a public demand they could not control, even if they had wanted to, continued, with increasing bellicosity, to scrape the bottom of the barrel for yet more colonial burdens for the white man to carry.

... [I]n conclusion, a paradox must be noted. Hobson's analysis of "imperialism" was defective: but the fact that it was defective was probably the result of his having grasped one essential truth about the imperial movement—that it had become irrational. Seeing clearly that the new tropical colonies could not be justified in terms of their economic value to the metropolitan powers—the criterion a nineteenth century rationalist would naturally apply—he was forced back on the theory that they must have been of value to sectional interests at least; and that these had succeeded in hoodwinking a presumably sane public opinion....

... [I]n the second half of the twentieth century, it can be seen that imperialism owed its popular appeal not to the sinister influence of the capitalists, but to its inherent attractions for the masses. In the new quasi-democratic Europe, the popularity of the imperial idea marked a rejection of the sane morality of the account-book, and the adoption of a creed based on such irrational concepts as racial superiority and the prestige of the nation. Whether we interpret it ... as a castback to the ideas of the old autocratic monarchies of the *ancien régime,* or as something altogether new—the first of the irrational myths that have dominated the first half of the twentieth century—it is clear that imperialism cannot be explained in simple terms of economic theory and the nature of finance capitalism. In its mature form it can best be described as a sociological phenomenon with roots in political facts; and it can properly be understood only in terms of the same social hysteria that has since given birth to other and more disastrous forms of aggressive nationalism.

ELIE HALÉVY (1870–1937), a major French historian, devoted twenty years to his monumental six-volume *History of the English People in the Nineteenth Century*. The initial volumes were developed from lectures in British history at the *Ecole libre des sciences politiques.* By the time he reached the fifth volume, *Imperialism and the Rise of Labour,* from which the following selection is drawn, World War I had intervened and Halévy was convinced that Britain had entered a gradual state of decline. He saw the evangelical movement as one of the major influences in transforming British society in the nineteenth century, but so too, he felt, was the rise of new techniques in mass journalism, techniques that promoted imperialism by creating a demand for jingoistic and sensational news.*

Public Opinion and Imperialism: The New Journalism

If . . . we examine the new imperialism . . . closely, we shall discover that, if the British were aggressive, it was because they believed themselves threatened. A peaceful nation the English had undoubtedly been in the period around 1860, possibly more peace-loving than any nation in the entire course of history. But these peaceable dispositions masked a profound disdain. Sure of her command of the seas and proud of her vast wealth, England scornfully abandoned the Continent to its dissensions. Unfortunately, the situation, not only on the Continent, where peace had prevailed for twenty-five years, but throughout the world, had radically altered during the last half century to the disadvantage of Britain. . . .

The British could still contemplate with pride the vast size of their mercantile marine, whose tonnage equalled that of all foreign merchantmen together. But what of the goods carried by these innumerable vessels? British exports for the year preceding the return of the Conservatives to power in 1895 did not so far exceed in value American, French, or German as in former years. Comfort might be derived from the consideration that, if the national production were to be fairly estimated on the basis of these figures, they must not be taken simply, but the value of the exports must be

* Excerpted from Elie Halévy, *A History of the English People in the Nineteenth Century,* vol. V, *Imperialism and the Rise of Labour,* trans. by E. W. Watkin (reprint ed.; New York, 1961). By permission of Barnes & Noble, Inc., New York, and Ernest Benn, Ltd., London. Original edition, in French, published in 1926.

divided by the number of the population. It would then be seen that Great Britain still far outstripped her competitors. The value of British exports per head of the population was more than double the value of American. But even estimated by this standard it must be admitted that the value of British exports had during the past twenty-five years steadily declined. The exports of the United States and Germany on the other hand showed a steady increase, and it seemed possible to predict with an almost mathematical certainty the day when Britain would be overtaken by these two nations. French competition did not inspire the same anxiety; like the population, the value of French exports remained almost stationary. Russian competition gave even less grounds for uneasiness. Nevertheless, Russia and France were extending their colonial empire in Asia and Africa and every area occupied by a foreign power was immediately closed to British imports by a customs barrier. The dissatisfaction inspired by the unfavourable economic situation had without doubt contributed to the Conservative victory at the polls. How did the Conservatives propose to remedy ills for which the Liberal policy had no cure? Their prescription was imperialism, the opening of new markets to British exports by the annexation of new colonies. . . .

Britain could well afford to import far more than she exported. Since she was receiving at the same time the interest of capital invested abroad, the balance of commerce remained favourable and the country grew wealthier. But several disquieting factors detracted from the comfort to be derived from this consideration. The great banking houses which controlled in London the investment of British capital were slipping out of British hands. Since the disappearance in 1890 of the celebrated firm of Baring, they all bore German, German-Jewish or American names. What use would they make of the sums entrusted to them by British capitalists? It was no matter for indifference if this capital was absorbed without return in some remote Argentine, as had actually happened during the previous decade or went to nourish the newborn industries of rival nations, Germany, for example, or the United States. Ought it not rather to be employed in developing the resources of the Empire, the Indian cotton mills, the large scale agriculture of Australia, the gold and diamond mines of South Africa and the Canadian foundries? The imperialists wished to guide British capital into the latter channels while at the same time making an outlet in the same direction for the surplus population of the country. In this way the capital of Great Britain would foster the development of lands which should be regarded as England overseas, Greater Britain. By contact with her young colonies the old country would renew her youth.

In those distant days when England was at war with the armies of revolutionary and imperial France, it was the fashion in Paris to declaim against the nation of shopkeepers, the insular Carthage which presumed to oppose the modern Rome. In reality the nation of shopkeepers at that period returned only a handful of business men to Parliament: it was represented and ruled by an aristocracy whose ample revenues derived from the rental of their estates raised them to a position of supremacy over the representatives of business. When therefore that aristocracy fostered on every sea the development of British commerce, its position as the defender of the national interests was the stronger, because it was impossible to suspect the ministers of defending their private interests or even the immediate interest of their class. What changes a century had brought! Business men of every description—manufacturers and merchants, directors of companies, mine owners, brewers, bankers—made up 250 members of the House of Commons returned in 1895, and the remaining members, barristers, officers, and gentlemen of leisure, were bound to the business world by ties almost as close. The gentry in particular, still well represented on the Conservative benches, could not dream of living on the rents of their estates. The fall in the price of all food stuffs had hastened the decay of British agriculture, and now landowners visited the country only to spend the money they had made in the cities. How did they make it? The enormous growth of limited liability companies enabled the old ruling class to maintain on the whole its position in a country thoroughly industrialized. It was estimated that since the statute of 1862, which had placed their legal position beyond dispute, joint stock companies had issued shares representing a capital value of £1,500,000,000, an amount, it was calculated, double that invested in French and German companies together. And this calculation took no account of the capital of the colonial and Indian companies. Every Member of Parliament was identified to some extent by his annual dividends with the interests of the great financiers by whom all these companies had been floated, and the latter did their best to tighten the bond by offering Members of Parliament a place on the boards of directors which managed their companies and even by appointing them Chairmen of the boards. . . .

. . . [I]t was the Conservative party which, at the very time when both in London and the provinces it was extending its control over the Press, created a new type of newspaper to meet the needs of a public more extensive and less educated than that which journalism had hitherto addressed. On May 4, 1896, the young Alfred Charles William Harmsworth—the future Lord Northcliffe—brought out the first number of the *Daily Mail,* a paper of reduced size and costing only a halfpenny.[1] The new paper contained no feature which resembled the carefully accurate information and well-informed argument which for over a century had been the glory of British journalism. There were illustrations, serial stories, political articles of extreme brevity, and large headlines which dispensed a hurried reader from the perusal of the text. And there was an abundant supply of sensational news items to tickle the popular palate—crimes, catastrophe, royal marriages and funerals, sport, naval and military reviews and wars. Harmsworth's venture was immediately rewarded by an unprecedented success. At the end of the first three months the *Daily Mail* had reached a circulation of over 200,000 copies, at the end of three years the circulation approached 550,000. . . .

. . . [An] undisguised determination of policy by financial interests might have been expected to excite public disapproval, and provoke an organized campaign of protest in the Press and heckling in the House. There was nothing of the sort. . . . No one desired to invest party strife with the bitterness and passion it possessed in contemporary France, and no one considered that the riotous scenes provoked in Paris some two or three years earlier by the Panama scandal were

[1] Two morning papers were indeed already published in London at a halfpenny—*The Morning* and *The Morning Leader* . . . —but they were not very successful. . . .

likely to raise the tone of French public life. Moreover, when all has been said, and the imperialist trend of public opinion which placed the Conservatives in office has been considered in its most commercial aspect, justice demands that we should regard it from another aspect, equally real. Not for a single moment could the imperialism of the government programme have awakened the enthusiasm of the masses, if it had been nothing more than a manifestation of commercial greed, and had not contained a very considerable element of idealism. . . .

. . . At the very time when we are witnessing what might appear at first sight nothing more than the expression of a purely commercial policy, we also witness in the realm of ideas the decline of the "morality of self-interest" or "utilitarianism" which had been so widely accepted as the philosophy of British Liberalism at the epoch of its supremacy. The great missionary of Free Trade, [Richard] Cobden, had professed the ethics of self-interest, and Herbert Spencer had embodied this ethical and political creed in a vast system of sociology based on the principle of an identity . . . of individual self-interest with the interest of society. But it was precisely the historic inevitability of this identification which in Herbert Spencer's native country was being questioned more and more widely thirty or forty years after his popularity had reached its zenith. The English neo-Hegelians, influenced by German metaphysics, refused to regard society as a mere collection of individuals. Far from it being true that society existed in virtue of individuals and for their sake, individuals existed only in virtue of society and for the sake of society—that is to say, in so far as society was the embodiment of the ideal ends—science, art, religion, whose pursuit alone gave value to the individual. Society, in Hegel's terminology, the State depository of all the moral traditions of the nation, the real State, closed to all interference from without, and admitting no society superior to itself, a veritable earthly god: this was the philosophy which in 1899 found powerful expression in a book by Professor Bosanquet, which soon took its place as a classic.[2] Moreover, the English neo-Darwinians drew from the doctrine of evolution conclusions very different from those drawn by Herbert Spencer. In a book whose success testified to the degree in which it reflected the temper of the period[3] Benjamin Kidd, a self-educated writer, developed the thesis that the quality which gives superiority to a species or race and ensures its victory over its rivals, is not reason, a critical and destructive faculty, but faith, the willingness to subordinate immediate to remote interests, the interest of the individual to the interest of society. Reason becomes useful to the race only when it has been brought into the service of faith. It was not to their intellectual but to their religious and moral superiority that the Teutonic races, the English and German, owed the ascendancy they had achieved over the Latin races, victims of their intelligence and individualism, for example Renaissance Italy and Revolutionary France.

From this point of view, however, men of letters are perhaps more significant than professional philosophers. They address a wider circle of readers, and are, therefore, more representative of their period. What then was the tendency which prevailed in English literature at this time. . . .? Very different from

2 Bernard Bosanquet, *The Philosophical Theory of the State* (London, 1899) . . . .

3 *Social Evolution*, 1894. In four years the book went into 19 editions. . . .

[Moore, Hardy, or Wilde] were the authors read by the general public, who must be regarded as the authentic interpreters of the prevalent outlook.

That fascinating writer Robert Louis Stevenson, who had settled in an island of the Pacific to die in voluntary exile, was amusing children and delighting adults by his stories of adventure and heroism in the South Seas. Joseph Conrad, a smaller artist despite his loftier pretensions, a naturalized alien of Polish extraction who had served for many years in the British merchant service, was beginning to make a name by his novels, which almost invariably told the story at once sublime, sordid, and pathetic of the white man in the Tropics at grips with the hostility of nature and the aborigines. The unfortunate Henley[4] on a bed of sickness and pain dreamed of battles, glory, and conquest, and, if his poems were too "select"—both in quality and quantity—to reach the masses, this was by no means the case with the works of another writer, the literary mouthpiece of the period. Young Rudyard Kipling, the son of an artist who was curator of an Indian museum, had begun his literary career by imitating the French novel, and had dreamed of becoming an English—or Anglo-Colonial—Maupassant. But soon, as he celebrated the melancholy of the British Tommy on garrison in Asia and hymned the greatness of an empire washed by "seven seas," he became by universal consent the unofficial poet laureate of British imperialism. And now he wrote—for children, was it, or for adults?—his "Jungle Book." He set his hero, the little Mowgli, in the world of beasts, and the beasts taught Mowgli the law of the jungle, which maintains the balance of species at the cost of a never-ending struggle, a truceless war. Must this struggle, this war, be condemned as evil? Not when it is the law of the world. The spirit of conquest and aggrandisement must not be confused with the spirit of hatred, greed, and delight in doing mischief for its own sake; it is the courage ready to hazard all risks which gives the victory to the better man. A species of Darwinian philosophy expressed in a mythical form was the foundation of a moral code, chaste, brutal, heroic, and childlike.

We now see the exponent of imperialism under an entirely different aspect. Far from appealing to the self-interest of their audience, they call upon them to sacrifice their private interests, even their very lives, in pursuit of a lofty national ideal.... [This ideal] was, in the first place, the consolidation—if possible, the federal union—of the British of the United Kingdom with the British in Canada, South Africa, and the Pacific, of one democracy with its fellows. In many respects this ideal was Liberal, almost Republican, humanitarian, and its pursuit was not ignoble. In the second place, it was the forcible annexation of a large portion of the globe neither inhabited nor habitable by white men. But experience had apparently proved... that tropical conditions did not admit of the spontaneous development of great independent civilizations of the European type. Where England did not install herself by annexation, other European nations would occupy the empty place. To stand aside was not, as the Gladstonians maintained, to refuse from moral scruples to share the spoils, it was a cowardly refusal to fulfil to the utmost of the national ability the noble mission of the European races to civilize the world, to refuse to bear what Kipling called the White Man's Burden.

[4] W. E. Henley was editor of the *National Observer*, 1883–1893 and author of "Invictus"—Ed.

Public opinion exists at many levels and in many states of cohesion. Opinion may be vague, based on rumor; it may be nostalgic, based on training and education; it may be highly directed toward one phase of relations with an alien people, as in color or race prejudice; it may be inchoate or articulate. The four brief selections that follow deal with popular attitudes as created by the English school, poetry, and popular literature. The first is by A. P. THORNTON (1921–), professor of history at the University of Toronto; two examples of popular literature, drawn from the works of RUDYARD KIPLING (1865–1936) and H. RIDER HAGGARD (1856–1925) follow; the last selection is by WALTER E. HOUGHTON (1904–), professor of English literature at Wellesley College.

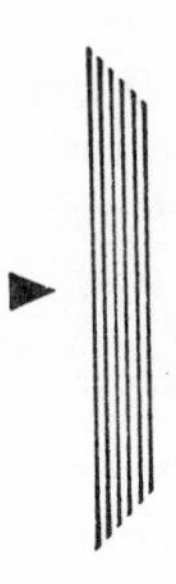

Sources of Pro-Imperial Public Opinion

THORNTON*

By degrees "the public school spirit" became one of the most potent of the imperial elixirs. St. John Brodrick (Lord Midleton), a "Soul"[1] who held many high posts in his public career, among them the Secretaryship of State for War and the Lord-Lieutenancy of Ireland, could declare in his autobiography—written in 1939—that no responsibility could ever compare with that of being a member of "Pop" at Eton. . . . Brodrick of course may not have meant this: but that he felt he meant it is of sufficient importance. At Eton, and schools that endeavoured to, but did not quite, match it, a boy's steps were set on the first part of that steady and inevitable progress towards positions of command over the majority. . . .

The emotional attachment to the ideas inculcated at such schools lasted a man all his life. It was a clan loyalty, like that which was devoted to Balliol under [Benjamin] Jowett, to Garnet Wolseley's staff "ring," to [Alfred] Milner's South African "kindergarten," and to the Middle East "club." Like all these, too, it was a loyalty devoted to the idea, rather than to any particular practice, of Empire. From such sects have always come the most fervent loyalists, who are loyal

[1] Related to All Souls College, Oxford—Ed.

* From A. P. Thornton, *The Imperial Idea and Its Enemies: A Study in British Power* (London, 1959). By permission of A. P. Thornton, Macmillan & Company Ltd., and St. Martin's Press.

not so much to a cause as to themselves, because they are the products and the representatives of a system and a tradition in whose context alone their lives have meaning and purpose. Men stamped in any of these moulds thought it the most obvious and natural thing in the world to pass on their view of the world and its ways entire to the coming generation. Since however there are always three generations alive at any one time, it is hardly possible for the outlook of the grandfather to be other than entirely alien to that of the grandson: it is usually only the sense of "good form" once more, that prevents the good grandson from pointing this out. But the ideals and the idols may still throw their shadows far: and so too, very often, do the books which embalm for ever the atmosphere that so kindled the imaginations of the age that has gone. Certainly the works of John Buchan and G. A. Henty were to stand in an honoured place on the shelves of all three generations.

Buchan, the Scottish "outsider" with his idealised admiration for the closed circle of English power, where everyone knew everyone else, where everyone knew where everything was—"the pass on your right as you go over into Ladakh"—and where everything and everyone not so known was not worth knowing, painted a better romantic picture of Empire than Disraeli, for all his coruscations, ever managed to convey of the world of political power. His books set the standards to which imperialists should conform: a straight and simple standard, but one which only genuine white men were able to follow: Henty, writing for a younger age-group, produced some ninety volumes which are no part of English literature, but are certainly part of the historical evolution of the sentiment of self-confident imperialism. The younger reader was enabled to identify himself with a hero who might accompany *Moore to Corunna, Wolfe to Canada,* might go *With Roberts to Pretoria* or *With Kitchener to the Soudan,* and win his imperial spurs with them all. In one's presence, indeed with one's active assistance, fortresses were stormed and arrogance brought low, dramatic rescues effected and the country's honour redeemed. All this was done in the fresh air, to a code that was always implicit in the character of the hero. Yorke Harberton, for example *(With Roberts to Pretoria)* was a typical public school boy,

> a good specimen of the class by which Britain has been built up, her colonies formed, and her battlefields won—a class in point of energy, fearlessness, the spirit of adventure, and a readiness to face and overcome all difficulties, unmatched in the world.

He is the stamp of all the Henty heroes, and very willing to read about his exploits was an audience composed not only of the young idea at home, but of the Services and the settlers as well, people who were often baffled by the more obscure of Kipling's imperial incantations. Kipling interested himself in the discipline of the imperial idea and its effect upon varying sorts and conditions of men; but Henty delineated only one type of character, and it was comforting for his readers to assume that there was really no other.[2] Henty's British Empire was the gentleman's patrimony overseas: his imperialists were never jingoes, politicians, or promoters. He never took a lad *With Barnato to the Diamond Diggings* or celebrated *A Venture in Argentine Rails.*

The influence of this kind of writing is of course impossible to assess accu-

2 And cf. Rider Haggard's *King Solomon's Mines,* which sold 5,000 copies in two months of 1885.

rately, but that it had influence cannot be denied. The "Greyfriars" and "St. Jim's" stories of Frank Richards were still, in the 1930's, reflecting the attitudes and ideals of the 1880's and 1890's. Their illustrations still showed a hero, wrongfully accused, standing in an approved Henty pose: serious, foursquare, right hand clenched across the chest as one who despises the knife thrust of the Pathan—he is, perhaps, being charged with stealing a postal order. (This is, of course, the predicament of Terence Rattigan's *Boy,* whose *Winslow* father (1947) is pure Henty.) It became fashionable to burlesque the Henty hero, but that it was thought necessary to do so proves how tenaciously his image of the Englishman, whom Santayana called the schoolboy master of the world, has survived. For it is the *rightness* of the careers Henty describes that makes them so impressive. It is right to have a strong sense of duty, to rescue the benighted, to help the weak, and to impose stern but just government. And the reward is plain, for Henty's books have as happy an ending as books can well have. His hero earns the respect of whatever great man he has attached himself to. He is conscious of having played some useful part in a great scheme of progress. Even if personally unfortunate, he has borne witness to the strength of a great tradition: a man may not always be successful in a quest *For Name and Fame,* but he will hold himself the straighter for having been *Through the Afghan Passes.*

Here was a point of view thoroughly in harmony with that of the Services themselves. The Service class that governed India, controlled Egypt, conquered the Sudan, and intended to make an annexe of Eastern Africa once the Government had brought out the company promoters, did not make use of slogans, or patriotic songs, or appeals to the flag. They held themselves commissioned to the Queen and to the country, and believed that they took a wider view of that duty than did transitory Governments at Westminster. They propagated this idea with remarkable success, not only among the public but in Cabinet circles as well. . . . In the Service view, political parties might be necessary evils at home, where there was a mass opinion whose weight had to be assessed, though it must never be allowed to obstruct paths of duty: but party interference abroad in matters that politicians did not understand, or wilfully preferred to misunderstand, was to be tolerated as little as possible. For was it not the soldier, ultimately, on whom the burden of Empire fell—the soldier who lost his life for its cause? Did this not give him rights not shared by others?

It followed from this, that the notion that imperial frontiers were national burdens was one that soldiers were unlikely to share. Officers had a vested interest in expansion: fighting the enemy, and then garrisoning his territory, kept them employed and brought them renown. An officer might genuinely believe himself and his profession to be above "politics," but nevertheless his allegiance was automatically given to the expansionist party—and he did not hesitate to make this plain. . . . Certainly, if an officer subscribed to a policy of inactivity, however masterly, he was binding himself to a self-denying ordinance which must hamper his military career. . . .

KIPLING*

THE ENGLISH FLAG

1891

WINDS of the World, give answer! They are whimpering to and fro—
And what should they know of England who only England know?—
The poor little street-bred people that vapour and fume and brag,
They are lifting their heads in the stillness to yelp at the English Flag!

Must we borrow a clout from the Boer—to plaster anew with dirt?
An Irish liar's bandage, or an English coward's shirt?
We may not speak of England; her Flag's to sell or share.
What is the Flag of England? Winds of the World, declare!

. . . .

A SONG OF THE ENGLISH

1893

FAIR *is our lot—O goodly is our heritage!*
(Humble ye, my people, and be fearful in your mirth!)
For the Lord our God Most High
He hath made the deep as dry,
He hath smote for us a pathway to the ends of all the Earth!

. . . .

THE WHITE MAN'S BURDEN

1899

TAKE up the White Man's burden—
Send forth the best ye breed—
Go bind your sons to exile
To serve your captives' need;
To wait in heavy harness,
On fluttered folk and wild—
Your new-caught, sullen peoples,
Half-devil and half-child

Take up the White Man's burden—
In patience to abide,
To veil the threat of terror
And check the show of pride;
By open speech and simple,
An hundred times made plain,
To seek another's profit,
And work another's gain.

. . . .

* From *Collected Verse of Rudyard Kipling* (Garden City, N. Y., 1924). By permission of Mrs. George Bambridge; Doubleday & Company; The Macmillan Company of Canada Ltd.; and Messrs. Methuen & Co. Ltd.

Take up the White Man's burden—
  And reap his old reward:
The blame of those ye better,
  The hate of those ye guard—
The cry of hosts ye humour
  (Ah, slowly!) toward the light:—
"Why brought ye us from bondage,
  "Our loved Egyptian night?"

Take up the White Man's burden—
  Ye dare not stoop to less—
Nor call too loud on Freedom
  To cloak your weariness;
By all ye cry or whisper,
  By all ye leave or do,
The silent, sullen peoples
  Shall weigh your Gods and you.

Take up the White Man's burden—
  Have done with childish days—
The lightly proffered laurel,
  The easy, ungrudged praise.
Comes now, to search your manhood
  Through all the thankless years,
Cold, edged with dear-bought widsom,
  The judgment of your peers!

HAGGARD*

At the date of our introduction to him, Philip Hadden was a transport-rider and a trader in "the Zulu." Still on the right side of forty, in appearance he was singularly handsome; tall, dark, upright, with keen eyes, short-pointed beard, curling hair and clear-cut features. His life had been varied, and there were passages in it which he did not narrate even to his most intimate friends. He was of gentle birth, however, and it was said that he had received a public school and university education in England. At any rate he could quote the classics with aptitude on occasion, an accomplishment which, coupled with his refined voice and a bearing not altogether common in the wild places of the world, had earned for him among his rough companions the *soubriquet of* "The Prince."

However these things may have been, it is certain that he had emigrated to Natal under a cloud, and equally certain that his relatives at home were content to take no further interest in his fortunes. . . .

Being well acquainted with the language and customs of the natives, he did good trade with them, and soon found himself possessed of some cash and a small herd of cattle, which he received in exchange for his wares. . . . Sending his cattle and waggon over the border to be left in charge of a native headman with whom he was friendly, he went on foot to Ulundi to obtain permission from the king, Cetywayo, to hunt game in his country. . . .

"Let him wait," said the king angrily; and, turning, he continued . . . discussion with his counsellors.

Now, . . . Hadden thoroughly understood Zulu; and, when from time to time the king raised his voice, some of the words he spoke reached his ear. . . .

Hadden watched and listened in amazement not unmixed with fear. . . . "We English must have fallen out of favour since I left Natal. I wonder whether he means to make war on us or what? If so, this isn't my place."

Just then the king, who had been gaz-

* From H. Rider Haggard, *Black Heart and White Heart and Other Stories* (London, 1900). Published by Longmans, Green & Co. Limited. By permission of A. P. Watt & Son and the executors of the estate of H. Rider Haggard.

ing moodily at the ground, chanced to look up. "Bring the stranger here," he said.

Hadden heard him, and coming forward offered Cetywayo his hand in as cool and nonchalant a manner as he could command.

Somewhat to his surprise it was accepted. "At least, White Man," said the king, glancing at his visitor's tall spare form and cleanly cut face, "you are no *'umfagozan'* (low fellow); you are of the blood of chiefs."

"Yes, King," answered Hadden, with a little sigh, "I am of the blood of chiefs."

"What do you want in my country, White Man?"

"Very little, King. I have been trading here, as I daresay you have heard, and have sold all my goods. Now I ask your leave to hunt buffalo, and other big game, for a while before I return to Natal."

"I cannot grant it," answered Cetywayo, " you are a spy sent by Sompseu, or by the Queen's Induna in Natal. Get you gone."

"Indeed," said Hadden, with a shrug of his shoulders; "then I hope that Sompseu, or the Queen's Induna, or both of them, will pay me when I return to my own country. Meanwhile I will obey you because I must, but I should first like to make you a present."

"What present?" asked the king. "I want no presents. We are rich here, White Man."

"So be it, King. It was nothing worthy of your taking, only a rifle."

"A rifle, White Man? Where is it?"

"Without. I would have brought it, but your servants told me that it is death to come armed before the 'Elephant who shakes the Earth.' "

Cetywayo frowned, for the note of sarcasm did not escape his quick ear.

"Let this white man's offering be brought; I will consider the thing."

Instantly the Induna who had accompanied Hadden darted to the gateway, running with his body bent so low that it seemed as though at every step he must fall upon his face. Presently he returned with the weapon in his hand and presented it to the king, holding it so that the muzzle was pointed straight at the royal breast.

"I crave leave to say, O Elephant," remarked Hadden in a drawling voice, "that it might be well to command your servant to lift the mouth of that gun from your heart."

"Why?" asked the king.

"Only because it is loaded, and at full cock, O Elephant, who probably desires to continue to shake the Earth."

At these words the "Elephant" uttered a sharp exclamation, and rolled from his stool in a most unkingly manner, whilst the terrified Induna, springing backwards, contrived to touch the trigger of the rifle and discharge a bullet through the exact spot that a second before had been occupied by his monarch's head.

"Let him be taken away," shouted the incensed king from the ground, but long before the words had passed his lips the Induna, with a cry that the gun was bewitched, had cast it down and fled at full speed through the gate.

"He has already taken himself away," suggested Hadden, while the audience tittered. "No, King, do not touch it rashly; it is a repeating rifle. Look——" and lifting the Winchester, he fired the four remaining shots in quick succession into the air, striking the top of a tree at which he aimed with every one of them.

"Wow, it is wonderful!" said the company in astonishment.

HOUGHTON*

[T]he Darwinians identified the economic struggle for existence with the course of nature. That the stronger should push the weaker to the wall was not only a cosmic fact, it was a beneficent process by which the nation got rid of its liabilities. As early as 1850 Herbert Spencer was happy to point out that the "purifying process" by which animals kill off the sickly, the malformed, and the aged, was equally at work in human society: "The poverty of the incapable, the distresses that come upon the imprudent, the starvation of the idle, and those shoulderings aside of the weak by the strong, which leave so many 'in shallows and in miseries,' are the decrees of a large, far-seeing benevolence." Small wonder that after *The Origin of Species* came out, Darwin read in a Manchester newspaper, "rather a good squib, showing that I have proved 'might is right,' and therefore that . . . every cheating tradesman is . . . right."

And, also, he added, "that Napoleon is right." For social Darwinism could equally justify war and militarism. It could give philosophical sanction to the chauvinism that grew up in the second half of the century with the increasing intensity of national rivalries and the scientific development of ever deadlier weapons of destruction. By the middle fifties the proud and combative John Bull was in the mood of boastful belligerance that welcomed the Crimean War. ... Confessing with obvious satisfaction that he feared he had a little of the wolf-vein in him and in spite of fifteen centuries of civilization, [Charles] Kingsley wrote off his *Westward Ho!* with maddened speed and called it "a most ruthless, blood thirsty book . . . (just what the times want, I think)." If he were only younger, he would be there himself, storming the Alma heights. "But I can fight with my pen still (I don't mean in controversy—I am sick of that. . . .) Not in controversy, but in writing books which will make others fight." ... It was British chauvinism (supported ... by elements latent in Puritanism) which by moments turned men like Kingsley and [James Anthony] Froude, [Thomas] Carlyle and [Thomas] Hughes,[1] into storm-troopers and led the British public to buy thirty-one editions of [Sir Edward] Creasy's *Fifteen Decisive Battles of the World* between 1852 and 1882 at least partly for the reason given by Spencer, in order to "revel in accounts of slaughter." ...

When this temper was reinforced by the arrogance of white supremacy, it produced some extraordinary fruits. It inspired Carlyle to write his article "The Nigger Question," and led to the defense of Governor [Elwood John] Eyre's high-handed and brutal treatment of the natives in Jamaica, in which Carlyle took a leading part. He found Eyre "visibly a brave, gentle, chivalrous, and clear man, whom I would make dictator of Jamaica for the next twenty-five years were I now king of it." In some circles it could even make Rajah [James] Brooke, the conqueror and ruler of Sarawak, a national hero, hailed with sentiments well reflected, I doubt not, in Kingsley's letter to [his friend J. M.] Ludlow:

> I say at once that I think he was utterly right and righteous. . . . "Sacrifice of human

[1] Hughes (1822–1896) was author of *Tom Brown's School Days* (1856) and *Tom Brown at Oxford* (1861)—Ed.

* From Walter E. Houghton, *The Victorian Frame of Mind*, New Haven, Yale University Press, 1959. Reprinted by permission.

life?" Prove that it is *human* life. It is beast-life. These Dyaks have put on the image of the beast, and they must take the consequence. . . . Physical death is no evil. It may be a blessing to the survivors. Else, why pestilence, famine, . . . Charlemagne hanging 4000 Saxons over the Weser Bridge; did not God bless those terrible righteous judgments? Do you believe in the Old Testament? Surely, then, say, what does that destruction of the Canaanites mean? If *it* was right, Rajah Brooke was right. If he be wrong, then Moses, Joshua, David, were wrong. . . . You Malays and Dyaks of Sarawak, you . . . are the enemies of Christ, the Prince of Peace; you are beasts, all the more dangerous, because you have a semi-human cunning. I will, like David, "hate you with a perfect hatred, even as though you were *my* enemies." I will blast you out with grape and rockets, "I will beat you as small as the dust before the wind."[2]

Plainly it is not the Malays and the Dyaks who have put on "the image of the beast" but Canon Charles Kingsley. Sadistic brutality of this kind is pathological, and no doubt the desire to "smash 'em good" in Carlyle and Froude as well as Kingsley had personal origins. But nationalism and racism, sanctioned by Old Testament Puritanism and social Darwinism, created an atmosphere in which the normal control of the beast in man could be seriously weakened.

[2] [*His*] *Letters* [,] *and Memories* [*of His Life*], [edited by his wife, London, 1879; New York, 1900,] I, 374–[37]5. Brooke was one of the two people to whom *Westward Ho!* was dedicated, appropriately enough. (Expanded note—Ed.)

From the seventeenth century and Shakespeare's *The Tempest,* many Britishers learned of their empire through its reflection in their literature. Now a new generation was reading of a new empire. Winston Churchill admitted to being influenced by Haggard's novels; thousands flocked to the boys' adventure tales of G.A. Henty (1832–1902) and the poems and stories of Kipling. Later John Buchan (1875–1940) would thrill much the same audience, expressing more fully than any of the others the "proconsular" idea. These writers saw things plain; their heroes, morally certain of the rightness of their acts, were idealistic free agents. They still were captains of their souls. The following examination of Buchan's ideas, by GERTRUDE HIMMELFARB (1922–) of New York, illustrates these attitudes.

The Imperial Responsibility

John Buchan—popular novelist, biographer, historian, Member of Parliament, and finally Governor-General of Canada—died in 1940, one of the last articulate representatives of the old England. He is the paradigm . . . of a species of English gentleman now very nearly extinct. The manners and morals celebrated in his books, the social prejudices unwittingly disclosed in them, and the attitudes and philosophy suggested by them have already acquired the faded tint of a period-piece. . . .

[I]n Buchan's novels . . . there is the clean, good life which comes with early rising, cold baths, and long immersion in fog and damp, in contrast to the red-eyed, liverish, sluggish, and demoralised life of the town. There is the casual bravery, classically understated, of his heroes. ("There's nothing much wrong with me. . . . A shell dropped beside me and damaged my foot. They say they'll have to cut it off.") There is the blithe provincialism and amateurishness of his spy-adventurer who complains that the natives in a Kurdish bazaar do not understand any "civilized tongue," of his Member of Parliament who cannot pronounce "Boche" names and confuses Poincaré with Mussolini, of the Cabinet Minister who will not be bothered to read the newspapers while on vacation. There is the penchant for sports that requires every hero (and every respectable villain) to be a first-class shot, and looks upon politics, espionage, and war alike as an opportunity to practise good English

From Gertrude Himmelfarb, "John Buchan: An Untimely Appreciation," ***Encounter,*** XV (September 1960). By permission of the author and Encounter Ltd.

sportsmanship: Richard Hannay, his principal hero, is much distressed at not "playing the game" when he abuses the hospitality of a particularly heinous villain; elsewhere he permits a German agent, plotting to spread anthrax germs through the British army, to escape rather than ignobly shoot him in the back; and another hero, Sandy Arbuthnot, during a tremendous cavalry attack involving Cossack, Turkish, German, and British troops, can be heard crying, "Oh, well done our side!"...

The most serious item in Richard Usborne's indictment of Buchan (in his *Clubland Heroes*)[1] is Buchan's preoccupation with success, his top-of-the-form ethic. A dinner-party in a Buchan novel assembles a typical assortment of guests: Bonson Jane "had been a noted sportsman and was still a fine polo player; his name was a household word in Europe for his work in international finance... it was rumoured that in the same week he had been offered the Secretaryship of State, the Presidency of an ancient University, and the control of a great industrial corporation;" Simon Ravelstone is president of "one of the chief banking houses in the world;" his son is "making a big name for himself in lung surgery;" and another guest is "about our foremost pundit... there were few men alive who were his equals in classical scholarship." So closed is the universe inhabited by these Calvinist-minded characters that they can agree to the precise rank and order of their success. Thus Sandy Arbuthnot is "one of the two or three most intelligent people in the world," Julius Victor is the "richest man in the world," Medina is the "best shot in England after His Majesty," Castor is the "greatest *agent-provocateur* in history," and there is one of whom it is said, with a fine conjunction of precision and vagueness, that "there aren't five men in the United States whose repute stands higher."

Yet closer attention to the novels suggests that these marks of success are not the ends towards which his heroes—or villains—strive. They are the preconditions of their being heroes or villains at all, much as the characters in fairy tales are always the most beautiful, the most exalted, the most wicked of their kind. They are the starting points for romance, not the termination. Indeed the theme of the more interesting of the novels is the *ennui* or *tœdium vitæ* which afflicts precisely those who have attained the highest state—and because they have attained that state....

The portraits of Montrose and Cromwell, in Buchan's excellent biographies, are... tributes to the complicated man who is torn by conflicting ideas and emotions and barely manages to maintain a precarious balance.... They were sensitive souls, fated to noble failures and pyrrhic victories....

The English intellectual of Buchan's generation was loath to parade his intelligence; his Double First at the university had to be acquired without visible swotting or cramming. (Buchan's characters never admitted to memorising anything; they had "fly-paper memories" to which long passages of poetry or facts adhered effortlessly.) And his writing suggested not the anguish of creation but the casualness of civilised conversation. In this relaxed manner, Buchan was able to produce fifty-seven books in the interstices of his other more absorbing occupations—the law, interrupted by a short period of service with Milner in South Africa, then business, Parliament, and finally the Governor-Generalship of Canada.

Such productivity could only be at-

1 (London, 1953)—Ed.

tained if one wrote not merely *as* one spoke, but also *what* one spoke. This is the real clue to Buchan's (as to the Victorians') prodigious output. There are many to-day who are as rich in intellectual resources; there are few who feel so free to draw upon their capital. Buchan had confidence not only in his knowledge, but also in his opinions, attitudes, intuitions, and prejudices. What he wrote for the public was what he felt in private; he did not think to labour for a subtlety or profundity that did not come spontaneously, or to censor his spontaneous thoughts before committing them to paper. He had none of the scruples that are so inhibiting to-day. He was candid about race, nation, religion, and class, because it did not occur to him that anything he was capable of feeling or thinking could be reprehensible. His creative strength was the strength of his character. . . .

It would be almost impossible to reissue in America to-day one of his earliest and most successful novels, *Prester John,* first published in 1910 and for decades an enormously popular boy's book. *Prester John* is the story of a native African uprising led by a Western-educated Negro who seeks to harness the primitive religion and nationalism of the savages to set himself up as the demi-god of a native republic. If this theme is calculated to outrage the liberal, Buchan's language—the hero, a white boy, speaks of "niggers" with their "preposterous negro lineaments"—does nothing to mitigate the offence. Yet his racism, while a doctrine of inequality, is not a counsel of inhumanity. Laputa, the native leader, is represented as a noble figure and worthy antagonist. When he is defeated in honourable battle, the classical note of the White Man's Burden is sounded:

> I knew then the meaning of the white man's duty. He has to take all risks, recking nothing of his life or his fortunes and well content to find his reward in the fulfilment of his task. That is the difference between white and black, the gift of responsibility, the power of being in a little way a king; and so long as we know this and practise it, we will rule not in Africa alone but wherever there are dark men who live only for the day and for their own bellies. Moreover, the work made me pitiful and kindly. I learned much of the untold grievances of the natives and saw something of their strange, twisted reasoning.

Prester John was one of Buchan's earliest and least mature books, or possibly the fact that it was intended as a boy's book was responsible for the shrillness of its message. Elsewhere the racism was more a matter of instinct and sentiment than of ideology or doctrine. Buchan was not conscious of race as a "problem" to which racism provided a solution. . . .

In spite of the usual protestation, to explain is, in large measure, to excuse. The familiar racist sentiments of Buchan, Kipling, even Conrad, were a reflection of a common attitude. They were descriptive, not prescriptive; not an incitement to novel political action, but an attempt to express differences of culture and colour in terms that had been unquestioned for generations. To-day, when differences of race have attained the status of problems—and tragic problems—writers with the best of motives and finest of sensibilities must often take refuge in evasion and subterfuge. Neutral, scientific words replace the old charged ones, and then, because even the neutral ones—"Negro" in place of "nigger"—give offence, in testifying to differences that men of goodwill would prefer forgotten, disingenuous euphemisms are invented—"non-white" in place of "Negro." It is at this stage that one may find a virtue of sorts in Buchan: the virtue of candour, which has both an aesthetic and an ethical appeal....

If Buchan's attitude to race and class is apt to cause dismay, his attitude to nation and empire may be even more distressing. "For King and Country," the homily of generations of housemasters, is taken to be the ... message of his work. Few to-day can sympathise with his own retrospect of the imperial vision:

> I dreamed of a world-wide brotherhood with the background of a common race and creed, consecrated to the service of peace; Britain enriching the rest out of her culture and traditions, and the spirit of the Dominions like a strong wind freshening the stuffiness of the old lands.

This ideal is commonly regarded to-day as a utopian fantasy. But Buchan himself was no innocent, and when he confessed to his dream it was with the knowledge that his words had become irredeemable platitudes. "The 'white man's burden,'" he complained towards the end of his life, "is now an almost meaningless phrase; then it involved a new philosophy of politics, and an ethical standard, serious and surely not ignoble."

If there was rhetoric and fancy in the imperialist circles around Milner, there was also a truth and grandeur which to-day is too little appreciated. In the biography of Cromwell, Buchan quoted Captain John Smith: "The greatest honour that ever belonged to the greatest monarchs was the enlarging of their dominions and erecting Commonweals"; and Harrington: "You cannot plant an oak in a flower-pot; she must have earth for her roots, and heaven for her branches." This is not to say that the imperial enterprise is always honourable; there are other motives and sentiments inspiring civilised communities that inhibit the impulse to greatness. But to deny the worthiness of the impulse as such is to have a crabbed view of both the past and the present. A respect for the integrity and independence of others is admirable, but so is a respect and faith in oneself; and while the missionary or proselytising temperament is to be suspected and feared, it is also, on occasion, to be esteemed. If self-serving motives are attributed to the imperialists, they can also be attributed to the "Little-Englanders," as was demonstrated by Raymond Asquith[2] in a letter to Buchan, in which he rued the day England had let herself in for an empire:

> If only Englishmen had known their Aeschylus a little better they wouldn't have bustled about the world appropriating things. A gentleman may make a large fortune, but only a cad can look after it. It would have been so much pleasanter to live in a small community who knew Greek and played games and washed themselves.

The dilemma of the imperial ideal was also the dilemma of the national ideal. Here, too, Buchan had a finer sensibility, and at the same time a broader sympathy, than he and his kind have generally been credited with. Thus he did not finally decide between the creeds of Cromwell and Montrose: Cromwell, as Buchan saw it, seeking to create a "spiritualised and dedicated" nation; Montrose satisfied with a homely, modest, judicious government of checks and balances. He saw the glory of the first, but he realised that men might become satiated with high communal, as with high spiritual, ideals, and might prefer to devote themselves to their private concerns. He did not pretend that the first path was without its dangers, or the second without its virtues.

[2] Raymond Asquith, eldest son of H. H. Asquith, British prime minister from 1908–1916, was a close friend of Buchan's—Ed.

While not yet fully understood, it generally is recognized today that racial prejudice—the conviction of a God-ordained superiority of one race over another or all others—played an important role in imperial expansion. Prejudice often found its expression in the idea of Kipling's "white man's burden" and thus had humanitarian overtones; all too often such convictions of cultural, national, and racial superiority found expression in a sense of power, of pure dominance. The link between race, the will to power, and imperialism is explored briefly by RENÉ MAUNIER (1887–), for years a professor at the University of Paris, in the following selection, taken from the first volume of a two-volume study of "the sociology of colonies."*

The Imperial Race

Power-imperialism is, in a word, the wish to dominate for the sake of dominating: the "will to power" as Nietzsche called it. This is no doubt an archaic phenomenon. "Primitive" tribes display a passion for conquering just for the pleasure of conquering, of ruling for the sake of ruling. It is this passion which underlies the lust for power, a mania and a rage which the moralists condemn. Hobbes called it "the desire for power," . . . and Saint-Cyran[1] coined the happy term "the spirit of primacy" (*esprit de principauté*). This feeling of "amour-propre," that is to say an active and personal *egotism,* in La Rochefoucauld's meaning of the term, may also be a collective egotism, which may be reinforced by and blended with a real craving for *cruelty:* imperial and imperious are one and the same thing. When this manifests itself not merely in the individual, but in the collectivity, and more particularly in the nation, we have power-imperialism or *collective amour-propre.* . . . Power-imperialism may take two forms, may wear two aspects: the personal and the collective. For this passion may rise to a delirious height in the case of an individual—the most outstanding example being Napoleon—the passion of ruling for the sake of ruling, of aggrandisement for the sake of aggrandisement. But

[1] Saint-Cyran (1581–1643) was a popularizer of the Jansenist religious teachings which placed emphasis on conversion and predestination—Ed.

* From René Maunier, *The Sociology of Colonies: An Introduction to the Study of Race Contact,* ed. and trans. by E. O. Lorimer (London, 1949). By permission of Routledge & Kegan Paul Ltd.

every human group has in some degree a collective desire for glory and for power. Amongst Greeks and Romans Victory was a Goddess; *Athena, Victoria,* is Power first and only later Wisdom.... Collective pride, or national pride, is a characteristic of every human society.

National pride is lust for greatness and lust for power: it is *collective dynamism:* the joy in force is in itself a good. Amongst writers it is those who exalt energy, men like Stendhal and Nietzsche, who have been best able to note and render the distinctive characteristics of this phenomenon, and who have told us how—for good or ill—the nations become possessed by this passion for command. They show us imperialism in its narrowest meaning, in its true meaning; as an instinct which itself supplies its own aim and its own driving power. There is, however, no breach of continuity between power-imperialism, spiritual imperialism, and cultural imperialism, for, as we shall see, all three derive their inspiration from one first principle, the idea of the purity of peoples and races. The idea of their own purity carries the idea of their election and their predestined domination, decreed by God, whose designs are to the human mind inscrutable. This idea of *purity,* which came to be secularised one day, as it is in our time ... proceeded from another idea, that of *holiness;* from a second idea, too, from that of *primacy* and quality. *Holiness* has been, as we know, the basis of spiritual imperialism; *primacy,* as we also know, the basis of cultural imperialism. These two concepts sloughed their original characteristics, their essential colour as it were, to merge in the concept of purity, the source and inspiration of every form of imperial pride. It is the pure peoples, the great peoples, who are by God endued with the mission of commanding, for the sake of commanding, to the benefit—*incidentally!*—of the whole human race. Pride, however, must inevitably precede benefit. Hence the appetite for command which assails those who crave command of distant countries.... Cecil Rhodes studied Cæsar's life; he liked to picture himself as emperor!

So it is true, as Stendhal said, that power is *the greatest of all pleasures.* Auguste Comte too in his *Call to Conservatives* speaks of the *need to dominate* and the *need to win approval.* And Auguste Blanqui[2] in his *Social Critique* denounces Man's "native impulse to invade" and his "universal thirst for usurpation." Let us, on the other hand, realise that another idea informs the dominating mind; if Nations and States by exercising power gratify a common desire, if they thereby obtain a common pleasure, they also find therein a common vocation and a common duty. For power must display itself and assert itself. *Noblesse oblige,* we say; Power no less imposes obligation. Strength unexercised is lost; it must be used if it is to be preserved....

This being so, power-imperialism has its *attitude* and its *conclusion*—its *attitude* lies in the idea of the *Majesty* of peoples or of kings; the affirmation of their "greatness," which serves to prolong and to revitalise the idea of the holiness of peoples and of kings. This is the notion of *Glory* in so far as glory is distinct from salvation.... Its conclusion lies in the idea of *primacy,* wherein "power-imperialism" and "cultural imperialism" unite. It is the notion of the superiority of dominating peoples, but is no longer wedded to the transformation of the dominated; it ends by being

[2] Louis-Auguste Blanqui (1805–1881) was a French socialist and a leader in the revolution of 1848—Ed.

domination for the sake of domination; it sets out simply to found and preserve an *Imperium* as a thing of value in itself. Primacy serves as an argument for the dominator as much as for the reformer. I am the superior and therefore: I wish to *alter,* or simply: I wish to *rule;* I wish to *convert,* or simply: I wish to *enslave*....

...Progressing from theology to biology, we have quietly passed from a mystic to an ethnic concept. Purity of Soul, purity of Blood, bestow Majesty and lay the foundation of Primacy. The idea of Race thus blends with the idea of Rank.

...Some hundred years ago or so, this faith in the primacy of blood gave birth to three terms: *Latinism, Saxonism, Albinism.* This Albinism is the "doctrine of the White Man," extending his primacy over the entire world. The White Man, in virtue of being white, has the "burden" of ruling over the Non-Whites, even if they might be called civilised. It used to be the fashion to discourse on the duties of a King, nowadays on the duties of the White Man; in both cases, the first duty is to rule as a master over his subjects....

Carlyle was the founder of Albinism.[3] According to him the distinguishing virtue of the *Gentleman,* which ought thereafter to be sought and ensued by every man worthy of this title, is: power. He sings the praise of the *Ruler,* the man who reigns over others, the directing-man, who is the true aristocrat; the praise of the man who is able to find scope for his energy, able by exercising to confirm and renew it. In this he agrees with Stendhal, but he is the first to deduce from these premisses conclusions of an imperial nature. It is he who was the first to speak of "dominating" and of "dominated" peoples. It was he who preached a universal despotism, for the *virtue* and the *advantage*—to be attained at the same time and in the same way—of the white peoples....

Amongst the Anglo-Saxons, as amongst the French, there had nevertheless been growing for a hundred years another idea aiming at making primacy general and universal: power-imperialism which would thus rule the entire world. This was to be the White Man's rule, not the reign of the Latin or the Saxon or the German, but *Albinism;* in other words the claim of the White Man to dominate the Non-White. This is in truth *Universal* Colonial Imperialism. It is very striking in the Anglo-Indian poet Rudyard Kipling. In his poems he speaks both of the English and the French, but he speaks too of the White Man who has quality and he speaks of God who vows to end anarchy and barbarism in the universe. The "White Man's burden," the White Man's task is mission, right and duty; it is a White Imperialism, a real Albinism.

The anthoropologists had, however, formulated the doctrine a hundred years earlier. They used to assert the White Man's primacy and to predict the White Man's rule. In the earliest controversies about race...the opposition between white and coloured peoples and...the superiority of the white peoples [was stressed]....The idea of *subject races,* fatally condemned by their colour to subjection, [became] a postulate of anthropology....It is...particularly amongst the English that Albinism has flourished....

[3] Especially in *Past and Present* (1843)....

There were other motives for empire than economic, political, and diplomatic-strategic ones, as the old cliché, "Glory, God, and Gold," implies. The missionary impulse, whether directed toward conversion to Christianity or toward conversion to the British way of life, was a powerful one. The following two short selections examine the missionary, humanitarian, and evangelical desires to see the non-Christian brought into the fold. The first selection is from an article by JOHN S. GALBRAITH, a Glasgow-born (1916–) American professor of British Empire-Commonwealth history at the University of California at Los Angeles. The second selection is from an essay by GEORGE BENNETT (1920–), Senior Lecturer in Commonwealth History at Oxford.

The Humanitarian Impulse to Imperialism

GALBRAITH*

[T]he upsurge of evangelicalism in the late eighteenth and in the nineteenth centuries involved tremendous implications for British policy toward "backward races," not only within the British Empire but throughout the world. Those who were caught up by the fervor of the evangelical movement in many instances experienced the mental and physical anguish of a tortured conscience followed by the ecstasy of spiritual rebirth. The effects of conversion were often startling. It could transform a former slave trader into a clergyman whose message to the world was poured out in the hymn "How Sweet the Name of Jesus Sounds." The duty of the reborn was not only to cleanse the soul by prayer and good works but to witness to the benighted, and the great missionary societies that were formed at the end of the eighteenth century were expressions of this zeal for the conversion of the heathen. Cynics were quick to point out that the saints suffered from spiritual longsightedness, since their perception of social evils at the far ends of the earth was far clearer than their recognition of misery at home. Thomas Carlyle in *Past and Present* turned his fury on the maudlin sentimentalists of Exeter Hall[1] who wept at

[1] Exeter Hall, the London headquarters for several sects, was the symbol of the many British missionary and humanitarian groups—Ed.

* From John S. Galbraith, "Myths of the 'Little England' Era," *American Historical Review,* LXVIII (October 1961). By permission of the American Historical Association.

the injustices to the savages, but were unaffected by scenes in their own society which to him were abhorrent:

O Anti-Slavery Convention, loud-sounding long-eared Exeter Hall—But in thee too is a kind of instinct towards justice, and I will complain of nothing. Only black Quashee over the seas being once sufficiently attended to, wilt thou not perhaps open the dull sodden eyes to the "sixty-thousand valets in London itself who are yearly dismissed to the streets, to be what they can when the season ends"; or to the hunger-stricken, pallid, *yellow*-coloured "Free Labourers" in Lancashire, Yorkshire, Buckinghamshire, and all other shires! These Yellow-coloured, for the present, absorb all my sympathies. . . .[2]

. . ."[H]umanitarianism" in the first half of the nineteenth century did not imply a reordering of the social and economic hierarchy; it did not attack the validity of the immutable laws of economics. The "saints" were not unconcerned with evils at their doorstep, as Car[l]yle alleged, and humanitarianism did contribute to reforms which ameliorated the condition of the poor and, indeed, indirectly to the transformation of the society. But he was correct when he cried that they were stirred by the dramatic and the exotic far more than by subtle forms of injustice. Graphic descriptions of the horrors of the slave trade could evoke profound indignation, and attacks on legal slavery could produce a movement of power sufficient to cause Parliament to pass legislation to end such abhorrent practices. But the leaders of these campaigns tended to accept stereotypes of "black Quashee" and of those who oppressed him which bore no relationship to flesh and blood human beings.

The preoccupation of Exeter Hall was not with understanding; it was engaged in a crusade against evil, and understanding would have blurred the issues. This characteristic gave it the power to destroy the institution of legal slavery in the British Empire, but it did not give it the wisdom to cope intelligently with the more complex forms of racial problems that remained after 1834. The missionary magazines of this era are filled with descriptions of the essentially noble qualities of the children of nature whom the missionaries sought to win for Christ. One article, typical of many, appeared in 1836 under the title "The Humane and Generous Caffre," describing the heroism of a tribesman who had rescued a white child whose father had been killed by the Kaffirs during the war and had carried him to safety in Graham's Town. Despite this act of nobility, he was imprisoned as a spy. The antithesis thus represented of the virtuous savage and the ignoble settler was a standard stereotype which provoked the anger not only of the white colonists generally but of those in the colonial society who were most concerned with the welfare of the tribesmen. . . .

Even among the missionaries themselves there were those who condemned the "humanitarians" of England for their unrealistic appraisal of the nature of tribal society and their lack of understanding of the complexities of the settler-tribesman conflict. In southern Africa such views were frequently expressed by representatives of the Wesleyan Missionary Society. One of their most prominent missionaries, the Reverend Mr. W. B. Boyce, wrote that "the undiscriminating and unreasonable prejudice of a class of philanthropists in Britain, has thrown back the Kaffer to his former degraded condition as the vassal of a tyrannical feudal lord." The Wesleyan and the London Societies were at times in a

2 (London, 1843), p. 278.

state of open hostility to each other, and the advice they offered governors for the resolution of the "native problem" was frequently contradictory. The Select Committee on the Aborigines, which was dominated by its chairman Thomas Fowell Buxton, quoted approvingly from the sermon of one evangelical minister that "it is our office to carry civilization and humanity, peace and good government, and above all, the knowledge of the true God, to the uttermost ends of the earth." Those objectives were not necessarily harmonious, and the committee's report was of little use as a guide to policy. Indeed, it was virtually ignored.

Humanitarians could agree that protection for the aborigines should be afforded by the executive as representative of the home government and could not safely be entrusted to a local legislature; they were united in opposition to unjust seizure of lands by European settlers and to a labor system which would subject unsophisticated peoples to indefinite terms of servitude. They believed that the salvation of these peoples in this world and the next could be attained only through religious instruction and education. Their influence in defense of the aborigines was of great significance. They contributed to the emphasis which in the twentieth century was to develop into the principle of trusteeship; they appealed to the conscience of British society against what many of their contemporaries considered the natural law by which the strong exterminated or enslaved the weak; and the violence with which they have subsequently been condemned by white racists is a measure of their effectiveness. But the cohesion of purpose and political power of the humanitarians has been greatly exaggerated. The principles of "Exeter Hall" were so broad that their effect on specific decisions in imperial policy after the Emancipation Act was amorphous. The language of humanitarianism was conventional in the Victorian Age and was used by those who were hostile to the saints of Exeter Hall. Every respectable Englishman believed himself motivated by Christian principles. Colonel George Gawler, writing to the commander of his son's regiment, expressed gratification at the outbreak of a Kaffir war, which would give the young man an opportunity to do his duty, and concluded, "I have always laboured to impress upon him that, whether in or out of the Army, 'the Christian is the highest style of man'; and I am grateful to God that my son, though far away, remembers my admonition."...

An individual in different situations might be labeled a "humanitarian" and and advocate of economy. Sir James Stephen has been described by his biographer as a "Christian humanitarian," and that description fits him as well as any statesman of his day. But in his counsel on policy in Cape Colony, Stephen advocated retrenchment with all the vigor of the most ardent disciple of Cobden and [John] Bright. Earl Grey at times expressed views indistinguishable from those advocated by the missionary societies, as when he sought to promote the organization of tribes north and west of the Vaal River for defense against the Boer, and on other occasions his policy seemed to be dictated by the Chancellor of the Exchequer. These differences in emphasis do not imply a contradiction in their philosophies. It would be a misconception to consider "humanitarians" and "Exchequer minds" as at opposite ends of a spectrum of opinion. Few nineteenth-century humanitarians would have been prepared to demand large levies on the British treasury for the execution of their schemes for promoting the welfare of "backward peoples"; they shared with the generality of the British middle classes a deep aversion to tax burdens for any purpose, colonial or domestic. They might contribute, and many contributed generously, in time and money to the work of a private society, but in their capacities as merchants, manufacturers, professional men, or landowners they expected vigorous economy in their government's budget. To the leaders of the humanitarians, as to Gladstone, economy was a religion.

Ministers showed public deference to the great missionary societies, and their dispatches were often couched in humanitarian language. But they could find humanitarian support for widely varying lines of policy. In South Africa some humanitarians opposed expansion; others supported the extension of British authority for the protection of tribes beyond the cape frontier. At times advocates of reduced imperial expenditures favored expansion and at other times retreat.

A great diversity of interests wore humanitarian garb. The Hudson's Bay Company professed to be promoting the well-being of the Indians; the New Zealand Company stated that one of its principle aims was advancement of the welfare and civilization of the Maoris. English residents of Port Natal before the annexation of 1843 called for the dispatch of imperial troops partly on humanitarian grounds—the protection of tribesmen against the heartless Boers—though there was reason for suspicion that their own self-interest was a predominant consideration.

Buxton's Select Committee of 1835–1837 opposed treaties with uncivilized peoples as a source of disputes rather than of mutual security; other humanitarians, including Dr. John Philip, superintendent in South Africa of the London Missionary Society, espoused such treaties. British governors professed to be following a humanitarian line when they adopted the treaty system in southern Africa. Whatever policy the government chose to pursue could be defended on the basis of humanitarianism. But the universal use of humanitarian language does not mean the universal ascendancy of humanitarian influences, and the humanitarians' own assessment is a most unreliable basis for determining their actual strength.

The "humanitarians" and their detractors shared a conviction that British society had a higher destiny than the extension of its physical influence. Victorians long before Kipling's reference to "the lesser breeds without the law" had a sense of moral and intellectual superiority, which often expressed itself as arrogance. But coupled with this conviction was an acceptance of obligation which even in an age of free trade and retrenchment was never entirely absent. British law, the most enlightened distillation of the best in the human intellect, was an article for export, and the conferral of British order, security, and justice was a priceless boon. Of this sense of destiny, the humanitarian movement was one, but only one, manifestation, and in recasting the interpretation of nineteenth-century imperial policy this broader "missionary" impulse must be given greater recognition.

BENNETT*

The Evangelicals made a . . . powerful contribution to the discussion of [one of the] main problem[s] of Empire: the rule of dependent peoples. The loss of America left the Empire predominantly one of conquest, no longer of settlement. This coincided with the rise of the eighteenth century Evangelical conscience.

Already in 1774 the problem had been broached in the discussion on the Quebec Act.[1] . . . But the French were of the same European Christian tradition; the issue was deeper, the problems graver in ruling India. Hence the importance of [Edmund] Burke's insistence from the beginning that all rule partakes of the nature of a trust. But a trustee holds a duty of more than merely allowing the growth of the child, of providing peaceful conditions for it; he must often provide the means of education. Whatever the virtues of the *pax Britannica* it was but negative; the finer Imperial rulers aspired to more. Thus Bentinck[2] in abolishing suttee for "the benefit of the Hindus" sought to persuade and carry Indian opinion with him. The tradition of British rule in India was with the Lawrences:[3] to preserve the peasant from oppression—an aim Cromer[4] carried over into Egypt—then to improve his lot by irrigation and famine control.

The two means attempted in the rule and education of dependent peoples have been entitled "direct" and "indirect"; the former by British modes and institutions, the second by working through those found native to the soil. In the period of the development of British rule in India there were some who sought the latter: Warren Hastings[5] investigated Hindu and Muslim law, Munro[6] as Governor of Madras maintained the *ryotwari* land-tenure system of South India, and supported the *panchayat,* the organisation of government at the village level.

Such an approach was not to continue. The Evangelicals opposed the presence of East India Company officers at Hindu temple-ceremonies, the Company being "the dry nurse of Vishnu." Indirect rule demands sympathy: this could not be in a ruler whose moral sentiments were outraged by suttee, thuggee, female infanticide, and the abuses of the caste system, all tolerated—as he saw it—under the cloak of religion. Moreover, the nineteenth century Englishman was convinced of his own righteousness and ability. Imperialism and self-confidence go together. In India the tone was set by [Thomas Babington] Macaulay who served as law member on Bentinck's council: himself the personification of the coming Victorian optimism, he de-

1 The Quebec Act of 1774 confirmed to the French Canadians their landholding system, civil law, and church within the British Empire—Ed.

2 Lord William Bentinck was governor general of Bengal, 1828–1835. *Suttee* was the practice of cremating widows on the funeral pyres of their husbands—Ed.

3 Sir Henry Lawrence and John L. M. Lawrence, the first Baron Lawrence, reorganized and administered the province of the Punjab after the Sikh rebellion of 1848–1849 failed—Ed.

4 Baron Cromer was British consul general and in effect ruler of Egypt, 1883–1907; he will be referred to in a later selection from Nicholas Mansergh as Evelyn Baring, his name before elevation to the peerage—Ed.

5 Hastings, governor general of Bengal, was responsible for many reforms—Ed.

6 Sir Thomas Munro was governor of Madras, 1820–1827—Ed.

* From George Bennett, ed., *The Concept of Empire, Burke to Attlee, 1774–1947* (London, 1953). By permission of Adam and Charles Black Ltd.

clared in his Minute on Education in 1835 the belief that "a single shelf of a good European library was worth the whole native literature of India and Arabia." The result of education in the English manner was necessarily that government, if Indians were to participate, could only be in the English forms—their education cut them off from their own tradition. A generation at least was necessary before they could take part; in the meanwhile British rulers and observers understood that the period of British rule was lengthened—"we are wedged in the oak that we have rent," commented Goldwin Smith.[7]

[7] Goldwin Smith, professor of history at Oxford, opposed expansionism and eventually moved to Canada, where he was an advocate of independence for the confederation—Ed.

The rhetoric of imperialism came from many directions: pulpit, penny press, stage, and book stall. This rhetoric was shaped by other sources: the scholar's lectern, the scientist's laboratory, the politician's hustings. The first selection below is by an historian, W.E.H. LECKY (1838–1903), who believed empire was the product of historical evolution. Social Darwinists thought in terms of another kind of evolution and BENJAMIN KIDD (1856–1916) saw British supremacy as scientifically natural. The oratory of empire reached its finest flowering in JOSEPH CHAMBERLAIN (1836–1914), colonial secretary in Lord Salisbury's third cabinet. Finally, since each speaks of India, an equally emotional statement by an Indian publicist, KUMAR GOSHAL, is included in rebuttal.

The Rhetoric of Imperialism

LECKY*
Inaugural Address, 1893

Patriotism cannot be reduced to a mere question of money, and a nation which has grown tired of the responsibilities of empire and careless of the acquisitions of its past and of its greatness in the future, would indeed have entered into a period of inevitable decadence. Happily we have not yet come to this. I believe the overwhelming majority of the people of these islands are convinced that an England reduced to the limits which the Manchester School [Free Traders] would assign to it would be an England shorn of the chief elements of its dignity in the world, and that no greater disgrace could befall them than to have sacrificed through indifference, or negligence, or faint-heartedness, an empire which has been built up by so much genius and so much heroism in the past. Railways and telegraphs and newspapers have brought us into closer touch with our distant possessions, have enabled us to realise more vividly both their character and their greatness, and have thus extended the horizon of our sympathies and interests. The figures of illustrious colonial statesmen are becoming familiar to us. Men formed in Indian and colonial spheres are becoming more

* From W. E. H. Lecky, *The Empire: Its Value and Its Growth. An Inaugural Address* (London, 1893). By permission of Sir Leslie Farrar, executor to the estate of the late W. E. H. Lecky.

numerous and prominent in our own public life....

It has been the habit of most nations to regulate colonial governments in all their details according to the best metropolitan ideas, and to surround them with a network of restrictions. England has in general pursued a different course. Partly on system, but partly also, I think, from neglect, she has always allowed an unusual latitude to local knowledge and to local wishes. She has endeavoured to secure, wherever her power extends, life and property, and contract and personal freedom, and, in these latter days, religious liberty; but for the rest she has meddled very little; she has allowed her settlements to develop much as they please, and has given, in practice if not in theory, the fullest powers to her governors. It is astonishing, in the history of the British Empire, how large a part of its greatness is due to the independent action of individual adventurers, or groups of emigrants, or commercial companies, almost wholly unassisted and uncontrolled by the Government at home. An empire formed by such methods is not likely to exhibit much symmetry and unity of plan, but it is certain to be pervaded in an unusual degree, in all its parts, by a spirit of enterprise and self-reliance; it will probably be peculiarly fertile in men not only of energy but of resource, capable of dealing with strange conditions and unforeseen exigencies.... Nothing in the history of the world is more wonderful than that under the flag of these two little islands there should have grown up the greatest and most beneficent despotism in the world, comprising nearly two hundred and thirty millions of inhabitants under direct British rule, and more than fifty millions under British protectorates; while at the same time British colonies and settlements that are scattered throughout the globe number not less than fifty-six distinct subordinate governments.

...There was a time when the colonies were so weak that they depended mainly on England for their protection; but, unlike some of the great colonising Powers of ancient and modern times, England never drew a direct tribute from her colonies, and, in spite of much unwise and some unjust legislation, I believe there was never a time when they were not on the whole benefitted by the connection.... Remember what India had been for countless ages before the establishment of British rule. Think of its endless wars of race and creed, its savage oppressions, its fierce anarchies, its barbarous customs, and then consider what it is to have established for so many years over the vast space from the Himalayas to Cape Comorin a reign of perfect peace; to have conferred upon more than 250 millions of the human race perfect religious freedom, perfect security of life, liberty, and property; to have planted in the midst of these teeming multitudes a strong central government, enlightened by the best knowledge of Western Europe, and steadily occupied in preventing famine, alleviating disease, extirpating savage customs, multiplying the agencies of civilisation and progress....

...Whatever misfortunes, whatever humiliations, the future may reserve to us, they cannot deprive England of the glory of having created this mighty empire.

KIDD, 1894*

The question that will . . . present itself for solution will be: How is the development and efficient administration of these [tropical] regions to be secured? The ethical development that has taken place in our civilisation has rendered the experiment once made to develop their resources by forced native labour no longer possible, or permissible even if possible. We have already abandoned, under pressure of experience, the idea which at one time prevailed that the tropical regions might be occupied and permanently colonised by European races as vast regions in the temperate climes have been. Within a measurable period in the future, and under pressure of experience, we shall probably also have to abandon the idea which has in like manner prevailed for a time, that the coloured races left to themselves possess the qualities necessary to the development of the rich resources of the lands they have inherited. For, a clearer insight into the laws that have shaped the course of human evolution must bring us to see that the process which has gradually developed the energy, enterprise, and social efficiency of the race northwards, and which has left less richly endowed in this respect the peoples inhabiting the regions where the conditions of life are easiest, is no passing accident or the result of circumstances changeable at will, but part of the cosmic order of things which we have no power to alter.

It would seem that the solution which must develop itself under pressure of circumstances in the future is, that the European races will gradually come to realise that the tropics must be administered from the temperate regions. There is no insurmountable difficulty in the task. Even now all that is required to ensure its success is a clearly-defined conception of moral necessity. This, it would seem, must come under the conditions referred to, when the energetic races of the world, having completed the colonisation of the temperate regions, are met with the spectacle of the resources of the richest regions of the earth still running largely to waste under inefficient management.

Exceptionally influenced as the British nation has been by the altruistic spirit underlying our civilisation, its administration of the Indian peninsula has never been marked by those features which distinguished Spanish rule in the American continent. English rule has tended more and more to involve the conscientious discharge of the duties of our position towards the native races. We have respected their rights, their ideas, their religions, and even their independence to the utmost extent compatible with the efficient administration of the government of the country.

The result has been remarkable. There has been for long in progress in India a steady development of the resources of the country which cannot be paralleled in any other tropical region of the world. Public works on the most extensive scale and of the most permanent character have been undertaken and completed; roads and bridges have been built; mining and agriculture have been developed; irrigation works, which have added considerably to the fertility and resources of large tracts of country, have been constructed; even sanitary reform is beginning to make considerable progress. European enterprise too, attracted by security and integrity in the government,

* From Benjamin Kidd, *Social Evolution*, Methuen & Co. Ltd., London, 1894.

has been active. Railways have been gradualy extended over the Peninsula. Indian tea, almost unknown a short time ago has, through the planting and cultivation of suitable districts under European supervision, already come into serious competition with the Chinese article in the markets of the world. The cotton industry of India has already entered on friendly rivalry with that of Lancashire.

The commerce of the country has expanded in a still more striking manner. In the largest open market in the world, that which Great Britain provides, India now stands third on the list as contributor of produce, ranking only below the United States and France, and above Germany and all our Australian colonies together. She takes, too, as much as she gives, for her exports to and imports from the United Kingdom nearly balance each other. In the character of importer she is, indeed, the largest of all the customers of Great Britain.... This exchange of products has all the appearance of being as profitable as it is creditable to both parties concerned.

... There is no question now of the ruling race merely exploiting India to their own selfish advantage. Great Britain desires to share in the prosperity she has assisted in creating, it is true; but, for the most part, she shares indirectly and in participation with the rest of the world. India sends her products to British markets, but she is equally free to send them elsewhere. As her development proceeds she offers a larger market for the products of our industries; but England has reserved to herself no exclusive advantages in Indian markets. Under the principle of free trade all the rest of the world may compete with her on equal terms in those markets. Our gain tends to be a gain, not only to India, but to civilization in general.

The object-lesson that all this has afforded has not been without its effect on English public opinion—an effect which deepens as the true nature of the relationship existing between the two countries is more generally understood....

CHAMBERLAIN*

Speech at the Imperial Institute in London, November 11, 1895

I will venture to claim two qualifications for the great office which I hold, and which, to my mind ... is one of the most important that can be held by any Englishman. These qualifications are that, in the first place, I believe in the British Empire—(cheers)—and, in the second place, I believe in the British race. (Renewed cheering.) I believe that the British race is the greatest of governing races that the world has ever seen. (More cheering.) I say that not merely as an empty boast, but as proved and evidenced by the success which we have had in administering the vast dominions which are connected with these small islands. (Cheers.) I think a man who holds my office is bound to be sanguine, is bound to be confident, and I have both those qualifications. (Laughter, and cheers.) I wish sometimes that the English people were not so apt to indulge in self-criticism, which, although it does no harm at home, is sometimes misinterpreted abroad. (Hear, hear.) We are all prepared to admire the great Englishmen of the past. We speak of the men who made our Empire, and we speak of

* From Joseph Chamberlain, *Foreign and Colonial Speeches* (London, 1897). By permission of the Trustees of Joseph Chamberlain's works.

them as heroes as great as any that have lived in the pages of history; but when we come to our own time we doubt and hesitate, and we seem to lose the confidence which I think becomes a great nation such as ours; and yet, if we look even to such comparatively small matters as the expeditions in which Englishmen have recently been engaged, the administrations which Englishmen have recently controlled, I see no reason to doubt that the old British spirit still lives in the Englishmen of to-day. (Cheers.) When . . . I think of the way in which in numerous provinces in India—and I might speak from my own experience of the administration in India—and I might speak from my own experience of the administration in Egypt—of the way in which a number of young Englishmen, picked as it were haphazard from the mass of our population, having beforehand no special claims to our confidence, have nevertheless controlled great affairs, and with responsibility placed upon their shoulders have shown a power, a courage, a resolution, and an intelligence, which have carried them through extraordinary difficulties—I say that he indeed is a craven and a poor-spirited creature who despairs of the future of the British race. (Cheers.)

GOSHAL, 1948*

With a few exceptions, imperialism followed the general pattern set by the . . . British in . . . India.

The condition of the people of India after more than a century of British rule beggars description. Only twelve in one hundred were literate, there was neither free nor compulsory education. The average annual income per head was 18 dollars. The Indian economists Shah and Khambata put it thus: "The average Indian income is just enough either to feed two men in every three of the population, or give them all two in place of every three meals they need, on condition that they all consent to go naked, live out of doors all the year round, have no amusement or recreation, and want nothing else but food, and that the lowest, the coarsest, the least nutritious." [1]

During the occupation of India by the British, industrialization of the country had scarcely begun. Ruled by highly industrialized Britain, the overwhelming majority of the Indians lived in mud huts in little villages, in unbelievable filth and squalor, reminiscent of the early Middle Ages in Western Europe. They made a feeble attempt at making a living by tilling a minute parcel of land, usually as a tenant farmer. They were ill-housed, ill-clothed, and undernourished to the degree that five to six million of them died every year from preventable diseases. Maternal and infant mortality rates were six times higher than those of England. Average life expectancy was 25 years. . . .

Within the part of India ruled directly by the British, political rights were doled out at long intervals in the shape of "constitutional reforms." The last such reform before the second world war was the Constitution of 1935, which proposed certain changes both in the central government under the Viceroy and the provincial administration under the governors. The central governmental scheme never went into effect. . . .

[1] K. T. Shah and K. J. Khambata, both of the University of Bombay, in *Wealth and Taxable Capacity of India* (Bombay, 1924), p. 253. (Expanded note—Ed.)

* From Kumar Goshal, *People in Colonies* (New York, 1948). By permission of Sheridan House, Inc.

JOSEPH A. SCHUMPETER (1883–1950), born in Moravia, was a professor of economics in Austria and Germany until 1932, when he came to Harvard University to remain until his death. Although he was well known as a theoretical economist before he was thirty, he also gained important practical experience while not yet forty as Austrian minister of finance (1919–1920). His best-known works are *Business Cycles* and *Capitalism, Socialism, and Democracy*. His essay, "Zur Soziologie der Imperialismus," first appeared in 1919; it was not well known in the United States until its publication in English in 1951. In this essay Schumpeter discusses the economic theory of empire and puts forward a psychological and sociological counter-interpretation, the idea of "atavism" in society.*

A Sociological Theory of Imperialism: An Atavism

[W]henever the word imperialism is used, there is always the implication—whether sincere or not—of an aggressiveness, the true reasons for which do not lie in the aims which are temporarily being pursued; of an aggressiveness that is only kindled anew by each success; of an aggressiveness for its own sake, as reflected in such terms as "hegemony," "world dominion," and so forth. And history, in truth, shows us nations and classes—most nations furnish an example at some time or other—that seek expansion for the sake of expanding, war for the sake of fighting, victory for the sake of winning, dominion for the sake of ruling. This determination cannot be explained by any of the pretexts that bring it into action, by any of the aims for which it seems to be struggling at the time. It confronts us, independent of all concrete purpose or occasion, as an enduring disposition, seizing upon one opportunity as eagerly as the next. . . . It values conquest not so much on account of the immediate advantages—advantages that more often than not are more than dubious, or that are heedlessly cast away with the same frequency—as because it *is* conquest, success, action. . . .

Expansion for its own sake always requires, among other things, concrete objects if it is to reach the action stage and maintain itself, but this does not constitute its meaning. Such expansion is in a sense its own "object," and the truth is

* Reprinted by permission of the publishers from Joseph A. Schumpeter, trans. by Heinz Norden, ed. by Paul M. Sweezy, *Imperialism and Social Classes*. Cambridge, Mass.: Harvard University Press, copyright, 1951, by The President and Fellows of Harvard College.

that it has no adequate object beyond itself. Let us therefore, in the absence of a better term, call it "objectless." It follows for that very reason that, just as such expansion cannot be explained by concrete interest, so too it is never satisfied by the fulfillment of a concrete interest, as would be the case if fulfillment were the motive, and the struggle for it merely a necessary evil—a counterargument, in fact. Hence the tendency of such expansion to trascend all bounds and tangible limits, to the point of utter exhaustion. This, then, is our definition: imperialism is the objectless disposition on the part of a state to unlimited forcible expansion.

Now it may be possible, in the final analysis, to give an "economic explanation" for this phenomenon, to end up with economic factors. Two different points present themselves in this connection: First, an attempt can be made, following the basic idea of the economic interpretation of history, to derive imperialist tendencies from the economic-structural influences that shape life in general and from the relations of production. I should like to emphasize that I do not doubt in the least that this powerful instrument of analysis will stand up here in the same sense that it has with other, similar phenomena—if only it is kept in mind that customary modes of political thought and feeling in a given age can never be mere "reflexes" of, or counterparts to, the production situation of that age. Because of the persistence of such habits, they will always, to a considerable degree, be dominated by the production context of past ages. Again, the attempt may be made to reduce imperialist phenomena to economic class *interests* of the age in question. This is precisely what neo-Marxist theory does. Briefly, it views imperialism simply as the reflex of the interests of the capitalist upper stratum, at a given stage of capitalist development. Beyond doubt this is by far the most serious contribution toward a solution of our problem. Certainly there is much truth in it. . . . But let us emphasize . . . that [this theory] does not, of logical necessity, follow from the economic interpretation of history. It may be discarded without coming into conflict with that interpretation; indeed, without even departing from its premises.

Our method of investigation is simple: we propose to analyze the birth and life of imperialism by means of historical examples which I regard as typical. A common basic trait emerges in every case, making a single sociological problem of imperialism in all ages, though there are substantial differences among the individual cases. Hence the plural, "imperialisms". . . .

Imperialism as a Catch Phrase

An example will suffice. After the split over the question of repealing the Corn Laws in the year 1846, the Conservative Party in England, reconstituted around Stanley, Bentinck,[1] and Disraeli, was in an extremely difficult situation. During long years of unbroken dominance, ever since the Napoleonic wars, it had at bottom lacked even a single positive plank in its platform. . . . Canning[2] was the first to grasp this truth, and it was he who created that highest type of Conservative policy which consists in refusing to shrink from the great necessities of the day, and

[1] Lord Stanley, fourteenth earl of Derby, was undersecretary for the colonies, secretary for war and the colonies, 1833–1834 and 1841–1845, and prime minister in 1852, 1858–1859, and 1866–1868. Lord George Bentinck was an ally of Disraeli in his attack on Sir Robert Peel and the Corn Laws—Ed.

[2] George Canning was Tory prime minister in 1827—Ed.

instead seizes upon them realistically and constructs Conservative successes on what would otherwise have become Conservative defeats. One of his two great accomplishments was his struggle for national freedom throughout the world—a struggle that created a background of international good will that was to mean so much in the future; the Catholic emancipation was the other. When Peel moved up to leadership, he could not follow the same policy, for his followers would have rebelled. He chose to fight against electoral reform, which played into the hands of the Whigs under Lord Grey[3] and helped them to their long rule. Yet at the height of his power (1842–1846) Peel did conduct himself in the spirit of Canning. He made the cause of free trade his own. The great undertaking succeeded—an accomplishment I have always regarded as the greatest of its kind in the history of domestic politics. Its fruits were a sharp rise in prosperity, sustained social peace, sound foreign relations. But the Conservative Party was wrecked in the process. Those who remained loyal to Peel—the Peelites—first formed a special group, only to be absorbed by the legions of Liberalism later on. Those who seceded formed the new Conservative Party, for the time being essentially agrarian in character. But they lacked a platform that would have attracted a majority, a banner to be flung to the breezes of popular favor, a leader whom they trusted.... Failure was inevitable under such circumstances, nor was it long delayed. Thus when Disraeli picked up the reins a second time... with a minority (1858–1859), he ventured along a different course. He usurped the battle cry of electoral reform. This was a plausible policy from the Conservative point of view. An extension of the franchise was bound to give a voice to population segments that, for the time being at least, were more susceptible to Conservative arguments than the bourgeoisie which did not begin to swing over to the Conservative side until the seventies. At first Disraeli failed, but in 1866–1867 he succeeded all the better.... Disraeli fell, but in the midst of disaster the essence of victory was his. True, it was Gladstone's hour. All the forces and voices of victory fought for him. But as early as 1873 it was plain that the meteoric career of his first cabinet... was drawing to a close. Reform legislation always brings in its wake a renascence of conservative sentiment. The Conservative election success of 1874 was more and more clearly foreshadowed. And what program did Disraeli, the Conservative leader, have to offer? The people did not ask for much in a positive way. They wanted a breathing space. Criticism of Gladstone's acts was highly rewarding under the circumstances. Yet some positive policy had to be offered. What would it be?...

...In this predicament Disraeli struck a new note. The election campaign of 1874—or, to fix the date exactly, Disraeli's speech in the Crystal Palace in 1872—marked the birth of imperialism as the catch phrase of domestic policy.

It was put in the form of "Imperial Federation." The colonies—of which Disraeli in 1852 had written: "These wretched colonies... are a millstone round our necks"...—these same colonies were to become autonomous members in a unified empire. This empire was to form a customs union. The free soil of the colonies was to remain reserved for Englishmen. A uniform defense system was to be created. The

[3] The second Earl Grey was prime minister from 1830 to 1834, during passage of the first great parliamentary Reform Bill in 1832—Ed.

whole structure was to be crowned by a central representative organ in London, creating a closer, living connection between the imperial government and the colonies. The appeal to national sentiment, the battle cry against "Liberal" cosmopolitanism, already emerged sharply, just as they did later on in the agitation sponsored by Chamberlain, on whom fell Disreali's mantle. Of itself the plan showed no inherent tendency to reach out beyond the "Empire," and "the Preservation of the Empire" was and is a good description of it. If we nevertheless include the "Imperial Federation" plan under the heading of imperialism, this is because its protective tariff, its militarist sentiments, its ideology of a unified "Greater Britain" all fore-shadowed vague aggressive trends that would have emerged soon enough if the plan had ever passed from the sphere of the slogan into the realm of actual policy.

That it was not without value as a slogan is shown by the very fact that a man of Chamberlain's political instinct took it up—characteristically enough in another period, when effective Conservative rallying cries were at a premium. Indeed, it never vanished again, becoming a stock weapon in the political arsenal of English Conservatism, usurped even by many Liberals. As early as the nineties it meant a great deal to the youth of Oxford and Cambridge. It played a leading part in the Conservative press and at Conservative rallies. Commercial advertising grew very fond of employing its emblems—which explains why it was so conspicuous to foreign (and usually superficial) observers, and why there was so much discussion in the foreign press about "British Imperialism." . . . [T]he plan had much to offer to a whole series of special interests—primarily a protective tariff and the prospect of lucrative opportunities for exploitation, inaccessible to industry under a system of free trade. Here was the opportunity to smother consumer resistance in a flood of patriotic enthusiasm. Later on, this advantage weighed all the more heavily in the balance, for certain English industries were beginning to grow quite sensitive to the dumping tactics employed by German and American exporters. Equally important was the fact that such a plan was calculated to divert the attention of the people from social problems at home. But the main thing, before which all arguments stemming from calculating self-interest must recede into the background, was the unfailing power of the appeal to national sentiment. No other appeal is as effective, except at a time when the people happen to be caught in the midst of flaming social struggle. All other appeals are rooted in interests that must be grasped by reason. This one alone arouses the dark powers of the subconscious, calls into play instincts that carry over from the life habits of the dim past. Driven out everywhere else, the irrational seeks refuge in nationalism—the irrational which consists of belligerence, the need to hate, a goodly quota of inchoate idealism, the most naive (and hence also the most unrestrained) egotism. This is precisely what constitutes the impact of nationalism. It satisfies the need for surrender to a concrete and familiar super-personal cause, the need for self-glorification and violent self-assertion. . . .

. . . Aggressive nationalism . . . , the instincts of dominance and war derived from the distant past and alive down to the present—such things do not die overnight. From time to time they seek to come into their own, all the more vigorously when they find only dwindling gratifications within the social community. But where, as in England, there is a lack of sufficiently powerful interests with which those trends might ally themselves, an absence of warlike structural elements in the social organization, there they are condemned to political impotence. . . .

Imperialism in Practice

What imperialism looks like when it is not mere words, and what problems it offers, can best be illustrated by examples from antiquity. We shall select the Egyptian, Assyrian, and Persian empires. . . . We shall find characteristic differences among them, as well as one basic trait common to all, even the most modern brand of imperialism—a trait which for that reason alone cannot very well be the product of modern economic evolution.

The case of Egypt, down to the Persian occupation, is particularly instructive, because here we see the imperialist trend toward expansion actually in the making. The Egyptians of the "Old" and "Middle" Empires . . . were a nation of peasants. The soil was the property of a hereditary, latifundian nobility which let it out to the peasants and which ruled in the political sense as well. This fundamental fact found organizational expression in a "regional" feudalism, an institution that was for the most part hereditary, rooted in real property, and, especially during the Middle Empire, quite independent of the crown. This social structure bore all the outward marks of force, yet it lacked any inherent tendency toward violent and unlimited expansion. The external situation ruled out such a trend; for the country, while easy to defend, was quite unsuitable as a base for a policy of conquest in the grand manner. Nor was it demanded by economic requirements—and indeed, no trace of such a policy is apparent. Throughout the period of the "Old" Empire of Memphis we learn of but one warlike undertaking (except for unimportant fighting on the Sinai peninsula). . . . In the "Middle" Empire of Thebes things were not quite so peaceful; still, fighting revolved essentially only about the defense of the frontiers. . . .

Things changed only after the expulsion of the Hyksos . . . in the "New" Empire. The immediate successors of the liberator, Aahmes I, already conquered upper Cush to the third cataract and then reached farther into Asia. They grew more and more aggressive, and campaign followed campaign, without the slightest concrete cause. . . . Why did all this happen?

The facts enable us to diagnose the case. The war of liberation from the Hyksos, lasting a century and a half, had "militarized" Egypt. A class of professional soldiers had come into being, replacing the old peasant militia and technically far superior to it, owing to the employment of battle chariots, introduced, like the horse, by the Bedouin Hyksos. The support of that class enabled the victorious kings . . . to reorganize the empire centrally and to suppress the regional feudal lords and the large, aristocratic landowners—or at least to reduce their importance. We hear little about them in the "New" Empire. The crown thus carried out a social revolution; it became the ruling power, together with the new military and hierarchical aristocracy and, to an increasing degree, foreign mercenaries as well. This new social and political organization was essentially a war machine. It was motivated by warlike instincts and interests. Only in war could it find an outlet and maintain its domestic positon. Without continual passages at arms it would necessarily have collapsed. Its external orientation was war, and war alone. Thus war became the normal condition, alone conducive to the well-being of the organs of the body social that now existed. To take the field was a matter of course, the reasons for doing so were of subordinate importance. *Created by wars that required it, the machine now created the wars it required.* A will for broad conquest without tangible limits, for the capture of positions that were manifestly untenable—this was typical imperialism.

The case of the Persians is distinct from that of the Egyptians in that the former appear as a "warrior nation" from the very outset. What does that term mean? Manifestly, a nation whose social structure is oriented toward the military function, that does not need to be readjusted to that function by the power of the crown and a new warrior class, added at some time to the previously existing classes; a nation where the politically important classes—but not necessarily *all* the classes—view warfare as their main profession, are professional soldiers, do not need to be specially trained as such.... [I]n a warrior nation war is never regarded as an emergency interfering with private life; but, on the contrary, that life and vocation are fully realized *only* in war. In a warrior nation the social community is a war community.... There is always an excess of energy, finding its natural complement in war. The will to war and violent expansion rises directly from the people—though this term is here not necessarily used in the democratic sense.... Hence the term "people's imperialism," which today is unquestionably nonsense, is in good standing when applied to a warrior nation....

Imperialism and Capitalism

"[O]bjectless" tendencies toward forcible expansion, without definite, utilitarian limits—that is, non-rational and irrational, purely instinctual inclinations toward war and conquest—play a very large role in the history of mankind. It may sound paradoxical, but numberless wars—perhaps the majority of all wars—have been waged without adequate "reason"—not so much from the moral viewpoint as from that of reasoned and reasonable interest.... Our analysis.. provides an explanation for this drive to action, this will to war—a theory by no means exhausted by mere references to an "urge" or an "instinct." The explanation lies, instead, in the vital needs of situations that molded peoples and classes into warriors—if they wanted to avoid extinction—and in the fact that psychological dispositions and social structures acquired in the dim past in such situations, once firmly established, tend to maintain themselves and to continue in effect long after they have lost their meaning and their life-preserving function.... The orientation toward war is mainly fostered by the domestic interests of ruling classes, but also by the influence of all those who stand to gain individually from a war policy, whether economically or socially. Both groups of factors are generally overgrown by elements of an altogether different character, not only in terms of political phraseology, but also of psychological motivation. Imperialisms differ greatly in detail, but they all have at least these traits in common, turning them into a single phenomenon in the field of sociology....

Imperialism thus is atavistic in character. It falls into that large group of surviving features from earlier ages that play such an important part in every concrete social situation. In other words, it is an element that stems from the living conditions, not of the present, but of the past—or, put in terms of the economic interpretation of history, from past rather than present relations of production. It is an atavism in the social structure, in individual, psychological habits of emotional reaction. Since the vital needs that created it have passed away for good, it too must gradually disappear, even though every warlike involvement, no matter how non-imperialist in character, tends to revive it. It tends to disappear as a structural element because the structure that brought it to the fore goes into a decline, giving way, in the course of social development, to other structures that have no room for it and eliminate the power factors that supported it. It tends to disappear as an element of habitual emotional reaction, because of the progressive rationalization of life and mind, a process in which old functional needs are absorbed by new tasks, in which heretofore military energies are functionally modified. If our theory is correct, cases of imperialism should decline in intensity the later they occur in the history of a people and of a culture. Our most recent examples of unmistakable, clear-cut imperialism are the absolute monarchies of the eighteenth century. They are unmistakably "more civilized" than their predecessors.

It is from absolute autocracy that the present age has taken over what imperialist tendencies it displays. And the imperialism of absolute autocracy flourished before the Industrial Revolution that created the modern world, or rather, before the consequences of that revolution began to be felt in all their aspects....

The floodtide that burst the dams in the Industrial Revolution had its sources, of course, back in the Middle Ages. But capitalism began to shape society and impress its stamp on every page of social history only with the second half of the eighteenth century. Before that time there had been only islands of capitalist economy imbedded in an ocean of village and urban economy.... Not until the process we term the Industrial Revolution did the working masses, led by the entrepreneur, overcome the bonds of older life-forms—the environment of peasantry, guild, and aristocracy. The causal connection was this: A transformation in the basic economic factors... created the objective opportunity for the production of commodities, for large-scale industry, working for a market of customers whose individual identities were unknown, operating solely with a view to maximum financial profit. It was this opportunity that created an economically oriented leadership—personalities whose field of achievement was the organization of such commodity production in the form of capitalist enterprise. Successful enterprises in large numbers represented something new in the economic and social sense. They fought for and won freedom of action. They compelled state policy to adapt itself to their needs. More and more they attracted the most vigorous leaders from other spheres, as well as the manpower of those spheres, causing them and the social strata they represented to languish. Capitalist enterpreneurs fought the former ruling circles for a share in state control, for leadership in the state.

The very fact of their success, their position, their resources, their power, raised them in the political and social scale. Their mode of life, their cast of mind became increasingly important elements on the social scene. Their actions, desires, needs, and beliefs emerged more and more sharply within the total picture of the social community. In a historical sense, this applied primarily to the industrial and financial leaders of the movement—the bourgeoisie. But soon it applied also to the working masses which this movement created and placed in an altogether new class situation. This situation was governed by new forms of the working day, of family life, of interests—and these, in turn, corresponded to new orientations toward the social structure as a whole. More and more, in the course of the nineteenth century, the typical modern worker came to determine the overall aspect of society; for competitive capitalism, by its inherent logic, kept on raising the demand for labor and thus the economic level and social power of the workers, until this class too was able to assert itself in a political sense. The working class and its mode of life provided the type from which the intellectual developed. Capitalism did not create the intellectuals—the "new middle class." But in earlier times only the legal scholar, the cleric, and the physician had formed a special intellectual class, and even they had enjoyed but little scope for playing an independent role. Such opportunities were provided only by capitalist society, which created the industrial and financial bureaucrat, the journalist, and so on, and which opened up new vistas to the jurist and physician. The "professional" of capitalist society arose as a class type. Finally, as a class type, the rentier, the beneficiary of industrial loan capital, is also a creature of capitalism. All these types are shaped by the capitalist mode of production, and they tend for this reason to bring other types—even the peasant—into conformity with themselves.

These new types . . . were freed from the control of ancient patterns of thought, of the grip of institutions and organs that taught and represented these outlooks in village, manor, and guild. They were removed from the old world, engaged in building a new one for themselves—a specialized, mechanized world. Thus they were all inevitably democratized, individualized, and rationalized. They were democratized, because the picture of time-honored power and privilege gave way to one of continual change, set in motion by industrial life. They were individualized, because subjective opportunities to shape their lives took the place of immutable objective factors. They were rationalized, because the instability of economic position made their survival hinge on continual, deliberately rationalistic decisions—a dependence that emerged with great sharpness. Trained to economic rationalism, these people left no sphere of life unrationalized, questioning everything about themselves, the social structure, the state, the ruling class. The marks of this process are engraved on every aspect of modern culture. It is this process that explains the basic features of that culture.

. . . Everything that is purely instinctual . . . is driven into the background by this development. . . . We must therefore anticipate finding [this true] in the case of the imperialist impulse as well; we must expect to see this impulse, which rests on the primitive contingencies of physical combat, gradually disappear, washed away by new exigencies of daily life. There is another factor too. The competitive system absorbs the full energies of most of the people at all economic levels. Constant application, attention and concentration of energy are the conditions of survival within it, primarily in the specifically economic professions, but also in other activities organized on their model. There is much less excess energy to be vented in war and conquest than in any precapitalist society. What excess energy there is flows largely into industry itself, accounts for its shining figures—the type of the captain of industry—and for the rest is applied to art, science, and the social struggle. In a purely capitalist world, what was once energy for war becomes simply energy for labor of every kind. Wars of conquest and adventurism in foreign policy in general are bound to be regarded as troublesome distractions, destructive of life's meaning, a diversion from the accustomed and therefore "true" task.

A purely capitalist world therefore can offer no fertile soil to imperialist impulses. That does not mean that it cannot still maintain an interest in imperialist expansion.... The point is that its people are likely to be essentially of an unwarlike disposition. Hence we must expect that anti-imperialist tendencies will show themselves wherever capitalism penetrates the economy and, through the economy, the mind of modern nations. ... The facts that follow are cited to show that this expectation, which flows from our theory, is in fact justified.

1. Throughout the world of capitalism, and specifically among the elements formed by capitalism in modern social life, there has arisen a fundamental opposition to war, expansion, cabinet diplomacy, armaments, and socially-entrenched professional armies. This opposition had its origin in the country that first turned capitalist—England—and arose coincidentally with that country's capitalist development. "Philosophical radicalism" was the first politically influential intellectual movement to represent this trend successfully, linking it up, as was to be expected, with economic freedom in general and free trade in particular. Molesworth[4] became a cabinet member, even though he had publicly declared—on the occasion of the Canadian revolution—that he prayed for the defeat of his country's arms.... [M]odern pacifism, in its political foundations if not its derivation, is unquestionably a phenomenon of the capitalist world.

2. Wherever capitalism penetrated, peace parties of such strength arose that virtually every war meant a political struggle on the domestic scene.... That is why every war is carefully justified as a defensive war by the governments involved, and by all the political parties, in their official utterances—indicating a realization that a war of a different nature would scarcely be tenable in a political sense.... No people and no ruling class today can openly afford to regard war as a normal state of affairs or a normal element in the life of nations....

3. The type of industrial worker created by capitalism is always vigorously anti-imperialist. In the individual case, skillful agitation may persuade the working masses to approve or remain neutral—a concrete goal or interest in self-defense always playing the main part —but no initiative for a forcible policy of expansion ever emanates from this quarter. On this point official socialism unquestionably formulates not merely the interests but also the conscious will

[4] Sir William Molesworth, secretary for the colonies in 1855, was a "philosophical radical" and opponent of transportation for criminal offenses—Ed.

of the workers. Even less than peasant imperialism is there any such thing as socialist or other working-class imperialism.

4. Despite manifest resistance on the part of powerful elements, the capitalist age has seen the development of methods for preventing war, for the peaceful settlement of disputes among states....

5. Among all capitalist economies, that of the United States is least burdened with precapitalist elements, survivals, reminiscences, and power factors. Certainly we cannot expect to find imperialist tendencies altogether lacking even in the United States, for the immigrants came from Europe with their convictions fully formed, and the environment certainly favored the revival of instincts of pugnacity. But we can conjecture that among all countries the United States is likely to exhibit the weakest imperialist trend. This turns out to be the truth.... [T]he United States was the first advocate of disarmament and arbitration. It was the first to conclude treaties concerning arms limitations (1817) and arbitral courts (first attempt in 1797).... In the course of the nineteenth century, the United States had numerous occasions for war, including instances that were well calculated to test its patience. It made almost no use of such occasions. Leading industrial and financial circles in the United States had and still have an evident interest in incorporating Mexico into the Union. There was more than enough opportunity for such annexation—but Mexico remained unconquered.... Canada was an almost defenseless prize—but Canada remained independent. Even in the United States, of course, politicians need slogans—esepecially slogans calculated to divert attention from domestic issues. Theodore Roosevelt and certain magnates of the press actually resorted to imperialism—and the result, in that world of high capitalism, was utter defeat, a defeat that would have been even more abject, if other slogans, notably those appealing to anti-trust sentiment, had not met with better success.

...[C]apitalism is by nature anti-imperialist. Hence we cannot readily derive from it such imperialist tendencies as actually exist, but must evidently see them only as alien elements, carried into the world of capitalism from the outside, supported by non-capitalist factors in modern life....

In 1952 MURRAY GREENE (1920–   ) wrote a carefully argued rebuttal to Schumpeter's sociological theory of imperialism while still a graduate student at the New School for Social Research in New York City. Greene's analysis was in response to an earlier article in *Social Research* which praised Schumpeter for having formulated "a rational theory of irrational drives." The views expressed in the article no longer fully reflect Greene's point of view, but they retain their internal force. While the following selection is directed to Schumpeter's theory of imperial causation, it also should be read with Maunier's views in mind. Dr. Greene is now managing editor of the *Encyclopedia of Philosophy* (New York).*

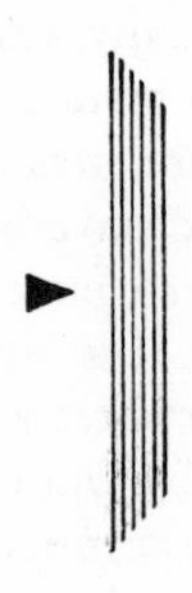

Schumpeter's Imperialism: A Critical Note

Despite its many brilliant individual insights, its sweeping historical range, and its bold and challenging syntheses, Schumpeter's thesis in his essay on "The Sociology of Imperialisms" is, to my mind, basically inadequate and misleading as a generalized theory of imperialism. It appears to me that the main burden of Schumpeter's argument is to show that capitalism is essentially anti-imperialist. To do this he develops a very specialized definition of imperialism which he then expounds with references to certain selected societies in history. He also sets up a very specialized definition of capitalism, which he then shows to be inconsistent with his definition of imperialism, thereby "proving" that capitalism is anti-imperialist.

I

Schumpeter defines imperialism as "the objectless disposition on the part of a state to unlimited forcible expansion." This disposition derives from a warrior-class social structure which requires "expansion for the sake of expanding, war for the sake of fighting, victory for the sake of winning, dominion for the sake of ruling."

One is immediately struck by how much is excluded by this definition. All instances in history or prehistory of ex-

* From Murray Greene, "Schumpeter's Imperialism—A Critical Note," *Social Research,* XIX, no. 4 (December 1952). By permission of the Graduate Faculty of Political and Social Science of the New School for Social Research.

pansion for the purpose of obtaining fertile land, grazing areas, hunting grounds, precious minerals, plunder, tribute, slaves, colonization areas, or commercial advantages are automatically excluded, because there was a specific object in mind. Also excluded, and most important of all for modern times, is expansion for the purpose of acquiring industrial raw materials, markets, capital investment areas, and cheap labor power. Because such instances of expansion serve a concrete interest they are not instances of imperialism. It is immediately apparent that Schumpeter's definition focuses attention exclusively on the internal compulsions of the particular expanding society, with no regard whatever for what it is that constitutes the object or goal, as such, of the expansion.

The onesidedness of Schumpeter's definition can perhaps best be shown by a comparison with the Marxist concept of capitalist imperialism. The Marxist concept also stresses the internal compulsions of the expanding society; and to a certain extent there is a similarity to the Schumpeter idea of limitlessness, in that capitalist expansion must press on and on, ever exhausting new areas of exploitation. But in the Marxist concept the relationship between subject and object is not meaningless. The subject has the need for expansion, but it is not just expansion for its own sake. The object of the expansion—markets, for example—is organically (dialectically) related to the specific needs of the subject. The expansion may be limitless, but it is not, like Schumpeter's, objectless, nor is it merely functional in a purely subjective sense.

Schumpeter's sole preoccupation with the subject is an abstraction of a portion of reality, and consequently a misleading distortion. Thus his almost ludicrous explaining away of British imperialism is not just a case of a particular miss which lowers an otherwise good batting average. It is a consequence of his subjectivistic approach, which necessarily excludes British overseas expansion—whether of the eighteenth-century period of commercial capitalism or the nineteenth-century period of industrial and finance capitalism—because in neither period could English society be termed a society based on a warrior-class social structure.

Schumpeter's additional qualification—that imperialism must be forcible—limits the definition even more. There are different kinds of force which states have applied and do apply against one another for the purpose of expansion. But Schumpeter means by force only military force. He must mean this to support his thesis. Thus one country's control of another through the superiority of its economic power (perhaps best illustrated in Latin America); the penetration of industrial products into native village or craft economies, and the shattering effects that this has on the economic and social structures of those economies (North Africa, the Near East, the Far East); the bribery or coercion of feudal chieftains or tribal leaders in an effort to persuade them to relinquish control of the labor power or resources of their domains (the Near East); the swindling of unsophisticated natives into bartering away their land and resources for trinkets, badges of prestige, or paper treaties (Africa); the forcing of loans on spendthrift or inexperienced governments, to serve as an entering wedge for foreign control (North Africa, the Caribbean)—these and other devious means cannot, by Schumpeter's definition, be termed imperialistic.

Even the threat of force—and more often than force itself this is all that is necessary—cannot be termed imperialistic, because, for Schumpeter, it is only in the actual application of military force that imperialism serves its true function for the subject. Thus even Roman imperialism . . . does not properly fit into his definition, for here the imperialistic actions, designed to strengthen the latifundian landlords' control of the state apparatus and to head off internal land reform, have not the same function as those in his classic instances of the Egyptian, Assyrian, Persian, and Arab Moslem warrior societies.

Is it not strange that the two imperialisms most important for Western civilization are, in the one case, excluded altogether, and, in the other, assigned an atypical, special role—and this in a theory that purports to be a generalized definition of imperialism? Why, then, does Schumpeter construct his definition in this way? Why must imperialism be "objectless" as well as "forcible"?

The answer is that Schumpeter's imperialism is a onesided, sociological phenomenon—the expression of a warrior-class social structure which fights because it is geared to fighting and has no other reason for existence. It is obvious that if expansion had a specific, limited aim, or if it were non-forcible, it would not necessarily fit this type of society. It could, for example, be an economic phenomenon and serve a non-warrior-class structure. Thus when Schumpeter comes to the analysis of capitalism he need only apply the following syllogism, inherent in his previous build-up: what is not the expression of a warrior-class social structure is not imperialism; capitalist society is not a warrior-class social structure; therefore capitalist society is non-imperialist. He then adds, to explain a few odds and ends, that what may look like capitalist imperialism just happens to occur in the era of capitalism, and is really only the remnants left from a past or passing age.

II

Let us now turn to Schumpeter's discussion of capitalism. Just as he abstracts from history a certain type of expansionism and terms it the true prototype of imperialism, so, too, he abstracts a certain type of capitalism and presents it as the true model of all capitalism.

Schumpeter takes the position that in capitalism there is no inherent economic drive toward imperialism. Tendencies toward economic expansionism he treats as coming under the heading of protectionism and monopolism. Protectionism and monopolism, he argues, are not endemic to capitalism, but are against its true spirit. They are opposed to the interests of most producers and of all consumers within the national economy itself, and are contrary to the interests of all nations as members of the international community. Where protectionism and monopolism exist, they are the outcome of the incomplete success of capitalism in its struggles with the monarchical power. . . .

As with Schumpeter's other ideas, there is some truth here; but, as elsewhere, the partial truth is used in place of the broader truth, not to supplement it. True, British capitalism of the latter half of the nineteenth century was featured by free trade. But was this because the British ruling classes were successful in their seventeenth-century struggle against the crown, or was it because the successful outcome of that struggle resulted in conditions that paved the way for British capitalism's initial industrial supremacy and its preeminence in the markets of the world? Of course the seventeenth-century political developments were important! But can anyone possibly maintain that British capitalism of the latter half of the nineteenth century would have been what it was if, instead of having had the field to itself in the early nineteenth century, it had been confronted from the very beginning by two such rivals as Germany and the United States? Or if, from the very beginning, it had started out as Germany did—having no worldwide empire, with almost limitless market opportunities already assured by political control, pre-established commercial contacts, and other ties? Of course Victorian England was a free-trade nation! But this was not because England had by then attained to "true" capitalism. It was because England had come first on the scene with the most; because the English economy could not have functioned as the industrial, financial, and trading center of the world without free trade. Where, outside of nineteenth-century England, has this "pure," protectionless, monopolyless capitalism existed at any time among the great powers?

This preeminence in world markets of nineteenth-century England not only explains, I believe, the free-trade character of English capitalism, but also affected the capitalisms which came to the fore later, and which, in their developmental stages, had to contend with the existing condition of English supremacy. It is significant, for example, that American capitalism, which developed unimpeded by monarchial power, and German capitalism, where the monarchical element was a factor, were both characterized by strong tendencies toward protectionism and monopolism.

In arguing that protectionism is a mere atavism, and that the logic of capitalism tends toward internationalism and free trade, Schumpeter generalizes on the basis of an atypical model and consequently misses the following basic points: that capitalism was organized along national lines and developed unevenly among the nations of the world; that this development was not smoothly upward, but was featured by fits and starts, including periods when factors lay idle and wanting employment; that finance monopolism played an increasingly key role as that development proceeded; and that these conditions made for an intensified economic rivalry among nations which was abetted rather than abated by the growing concentration of capital within nations.

In this connection it is interesting to note that Lenin, who was writing on imperialism at about the same time as Schumpeter, also contrasts Disraeli's famous remark of 1852 (on the colonies being millstones) with his attitude some two decades later. But where Schumpeter takes the position that Disraeli seized upon the cry of Imperial Federation as a happy slogan to revive the fortunes of the Tory party, Lenin interprets this change as a symptom that British leaders were already looking uneasily about for some insurance to preserve Britain's position against the growing menace of its more dynamic and efficient young rivals now coming to the fore—Germany and the United States.

Schumpeter's brilliant dissection of British party politics in the nineteenth century may appeal more to the scholar than the crude hammerblows of Lenin. But it is Lenin's imperialism which takes account of—indeed, makes into its central feature—the headlong international scramble of the capitalist powers in the final quarter of the nineteenth century to stake out claims in Africa, to secure strategic financial positions in the Balkans and the Middle East, to outmanoeuvre and outgrab one another in the Far East, a scramble that finally culminated in World War I....

III

We may now turn briefly to Schumpeter's argument that the sociology of capitalism—its social atmosphere, attitudes, and ideals—is antithetical to imperialism. Capitalism, he says, is rationalistic. It fosters democratization and individualization. It does away with blind loyalties to monarch, lord, or clan, and produces an atrophy of the martial spirit and the instinctive urge to aggression. Since capitalist rationalism stresses self-interest, and since imperialism is irrational and contrary to the interests of the majority, members of the capitalist society increasingly reject imperialism. In this rejection they are strengthened politically and morally by the tendency of capitalism to foster democratization and individualization. Furthermore, fighting is distasteful and unsuited to the bourgeois mind. The bourgeoisie, by its inherent disposition, cannot furnish the magnetic and forceful leadership needed by an imperialist state.

Now there is no question that rising capitalism leveled the weapons of rationalistic inquiry against the irrational (because outmoded) integument of feudalism, or that the development of modern science was closely linked with the rise of capitalism. But does this necessarily mean that capitalism as a system is rational? True, the individual capitalist has organized his equipment and technique of production along the most scientific lines. His bookkeeping is a triumph of cost accounting. And when he expands or curtails operations in accordance with market demands, he is certainly acting "rationally" in his own eyes. But rationally in relation to what? To a set of forces over which neither he nor anyone else can exert control, which has developed intensifying periodic crises, which keeps a significant portion of its human and capital resources in alternating states of enforced idleness, which tends to find solution more and more in production of goods that lie *outside* the "rational" mechanism of the market—namely, armaments.

... Is it not the "rational" capitalist era which has developed such rationalizations as racism, "the white man's burden," "manifest destiny," chauvinism, and the doctrine of "national interest"? If the world history of the last seventy-five years indicates anything, it indicates that the feudal age had no monopoly on incitements to war, that capitalism itself is quite equal to providing its own shibboleths and slogans to drag its masses into military conquest.

Much the same can be said of individualization and democratization. Early capitalism, struggling against feudal fetters, did foster these tendencies, in its own way and for its own purposes. Decadent capitalism, fostering an undemocratic concentration of economic and political power, bends the democratic process to its own ends, restricts opportunity, enforces mass attitudes, tastes, and conformities, and thereby negates its own early promises. The "individual," whom early capitalism liberated from the integrative feudal universe, is converted to a cipher. The individualization and democratization of nineteenth-century American capitalism, to cite only one specific instance, did not stand for a moment against the lords of the jingo press, whose efforts stampeded public opinion into a war with Spain in 1898—

a war that must be characterized as imperialist if the term is to mean anything.

Schumpeter presents the typical bourgeois as a man of preeminently peaceful disposition, preoccupied with his concern of making money, meekly envious of the lordly aristocracy whom he can never hope to emulate but upon whom he must depend for those qualities of leadership necessary for the functioning of the state machine. Is it not strange that this bourgeois group should, in one context, be described by the author as including the driving, ruthless, pioneering innovators, the daring organizational geniuses, the men of vision whose dynamic force propels all society along with them—and that in another context it should be described, when once outside its little circle of economic activities, as not capable of "saying boo to a goose"?

Here again is an instance of Schumpeter's seeing early capitalism as the ideal of all capitalism. Schumpeter's peaceable bourgeois did indeed exist. Balzac gives us a perfect insight into the typical early bourgeois, confined to his counting house, piling penny upon penny, once outside his shop cutting a comical and almost pathetic figure in the society of his betters. But Balzac wrote in the early nineteenth century. One need only contrast Balzac's (and Schumpeter's) bourgeoise of 1830 with the captains of industry of 1890 to see how inapplicable this early type is for the period of mature capitalism.

Schumpeter's thesis defining imperialism as the expression of a warrior-class social structure is untenable as a generalized theory of imperialism. Its inadequacies show up most clearly in its application to capitalism, the attempt at such an application resulting in a distortion of the nature of capitalism, including the positing of unacceptable supporting explanations, such as the atavism theory. Schumpeter's attempt to establish a theory true for ancient Egypt, feudal France, and twentieth-century capitalism results not in a generalized theory but in an unhistoric abstraction.

Smuts Professor of the history of the British Commonwealth and Fellow of St. John's College, Cambridge, NICHOLAS MANSERGH (1910–) is one of the leading scholars in the history of the British Empire-Commonwealth today. In his highly regarded *Coming of the First World War,* this author shows how noneconomic motives, largely political and strategic ones, contributed to imperial developments. Matters of primarily geopolitical import were central to Britain's involvement in the "scramble for Africa," Mansergh argues. His book grew out of a series of lectures on the subject delivered in 1944.*

Diplomacy, Strategy, and Imperialism

An age which has lost its faith is ill-fitted to pass judgment upon the age of Imperialist expansion. The sordid lure of easy wealth, the struggle for power, the lust for domination are motive forces well understood to-day, but the faith, the idealism, the passionate zeal to bring justice and civilization to the darkest corners of Africa, whose wretched inhabitants were the victims of Arab slavers, of pest and disease, are things of which little is now understood. Yet those easy phrases about the "Scramble for Africa" suggest only one part of the story, that part that does so little credit to the continent which claimed to be in the vanguard of civilization. The other is to be found in the lives of the missionaries, the early administrators and most memorably in the heroic journeys of the great explorers. In the pages of Livingstone's private *Journal* there is scarcely a page which does not betray his unshakeable belief that, wherever he went, he was watched and guided by his Maker. "You know," he wrote to a friend after the discovery of the Shiré Highlands, "how I have been led on from one step to another by the over-ruling Providence of the great Parent, as I believe, in order to achieve a great good for Africa." In the Chancelleries of Europe a constant pre-occupation with the struggle for power left men little time or inclination to think of achieving "a great good for Africa," so it is as well for the reputation

* From Nicholas Mansergh, *The Coming of the First World War: A Study in the European Balance, 1878–1914* (London, 1949). By permission of Longmans, Green & Co. Ltd.

of European peoples in the dark continent that so many of the explorers were so profoundly concerned with the welfare of the native races....

The opening up of Africa was the work not of governments but of individuals possessed of great courage and remarkable powers of endurance. There is something very revealing in that description by a companion, of Livingstone "tramping along with the steady, heavy tread which kept one in mind that he had walked across Africa." But where individuals had pioneered, governments soon intervened, and it is only with the motives that prompted their intervention that this [selection] is concerned. The political and economic importance of Africa was popularly overestimated. In Western Europe it was commonly believed that the acquisition of colonies was the high road to rapid economic development. Many writers, principally, though not only, German, failed, as Mr. Taylor has written, "to grasp the truth about the British Empire—that it had come into being as the result of British commercial enterprise and industrial success; and they asserted the reverse, that the prosperity and wealth of Great Britain were due to the existence of her Empire. The German campaign for colonies rested on the simple dogma—give Germany colonies and the Germans will then be as prosperous as the English."[1] Such popular beliefs may have influenced the minds even of autocratic governments, but they were not the directing force in overseas colonial expansion. The rulers of Europe thought primarily in terms of political not economic advantage and it was on the struggle for power in Europe that their eyes were always fixed. Expansion overseas was for the Continental States, not an end, but a means to an end....

Bismarck's sympathetic interest in French imperialism was an experiment on his side, in the possibilities of Franco-German reconciliation. That France should remain ostracized in Europe was his settled policy, but clearly it was not in the interests of Germany that she should be driven to despair. An outlet for her energies, preoccupation in colonial fields in which Germany had no interest, except for bargaining purposes, had everything to recommend it. The fact that, incidentally, French expansion in North Africa, and particularly in Tunis, would bring her into conflict with Italy, enhanced the attractions of this policy, even if it were not its primary purpose.... That Italy had already received German encouragement to seize Tunis must have heightened the Chancellor's satisfaction with French reactions. For his advice was heeded, and by the end of 1881 this former province of the Turkish Empire was securely French and Italy estranged.

Not only France and Italy but also England had traditional interests in North Africa. If it was the anxiety of the Third Republic to restore French self-respect after 1870; of a united Italy to raise herself to the level of a first-class Power by the acquisition of colonies on the southern shore of the Mediterranean; it was England's concern for imperial communications that led her with some reluctance to intervene in Egypt and so come into conflict with France. The Suez Canal of which control had been dramatically acquired by Disraeli was, as Bismarck admitted, "of vital importance" to her Empire being "like the spinal cord which connects the backbone with the brain." It was that fact that left England no freedom of choice. After

[1] A. J. P. Taylor, *Germany's First Bid for Colonies 1884–5* (London, 1938), p. 4.

"Dual Control" had been established in Egypt in the interests of British and French bond-holders in 1876, Lord Salisbury summed up the alternatives before his country. "You may," he said, "renounce, or monopolize or share. Renouncing would have been to place France across our road to India. Monopolizing would have been very near the risk of war. So we resolved to share." But it was not to prove as simple as that. Egyptian nationalist sentiment found a leader in Colonel Arabi Pasha, against whom no resolute action could be taken without provoking a popular outcry in France. Gambetta[2] urged the greatest sacrifices should be made to continue co-operation with England, but the Chamber was not prepared to heed his advice. So when nationalist riots broke out in Alexandria in June 1882, France withdrew and England acted alone. British rule in the name of the Khedive was . . . assured, and in 1883 Sir Evelyn Baring was appointed British agent and Consul-General in Cairo. . . . Despite the misgivings of Baring, General Gordon[3] was sent out from London as Governor-General with secret orders to carry out this evacuation, whose sorry sequel is a page in the history of England rather than of Europe.

England's task in Egypt was undertaken with German goodwill, which soon evaporated. Where Bismarck had once acknowledged comparative German indifference in the affairs of Egypt, he felt by the end of 1883 that the time had come when a less passive attitude would better serve his ends. "We are uncommonly grateful to Prince Bismarck," Lord Granville had said to Count Herbert Bismarck in January 1883, "for the friendly attitude of German policy this summer was of great service to us. Our being left with a free hand in Egypt we owe, when all is said, to Germany's goodwill. We are all aware that at a particular moment Prince Bismarck could have upset the coach if he had chosen to, and we realize with much thankfulness that he refrained from doing so." The price however had still to be paid, and in Egypt pressure was easy to apply. For the Gladstone Government, reluctant to contemplate annexation on principle, were left with no practicable alternative to acting as the nominal mandatory of the Powers. That left Britain in a weak and vulnerable position, for, of the Powers, France burned with resentment at her exclusion from Egypt, and Russia, without any direct interest in the Nile Valley, was hostile to the consolidation of Britain's position in the Eastern Mediterranean. This was a situation from which Bismarck was not slow to profit. The situation in Egypt made England, as Baring frankly recognized, dependent on German goodwill.

It seems clear now that Bismarck's colonial policy was more the incidental offshoot of tactical moves in Europe than a departure undertaken on its own merits. The price that Bismarck was most concerned to exact from England in return for German goodwill in Egypt, was some form of guarantee in Europe which would reinsure Germany in the West against French aggression. When it was made plain that this was a price that England was not prepared to pay he decided to explore again the possibility of friendship with France, founded on Franco-German hostility to England in the colonial field. That he was also influenced by internal political considerations is hardly to be denied. A forward colonial policy was well calculated to en-

[2] Léon Gambetta was the French prime minister—Ed.

[3] Charles George Gordon, "the finest specimen of the heroic Victorian type" (R.C.K. Ensor, *England 1870–1914* [Oxford, 1936], p. 81 n. 1), was killed by Mahdists at Khartoum in 1885—Ed.

hance the Chancellor's popularity at home.

... If Germany failed to obtain satisfaction for her claims overseas, the Chancellor declared that "she must try to gain closer touch with seafaring Powers, France included." But in actual fact the colonial grievances had been put forward largely because they might make closer co-operation with France possible. It was on the foundation of joint hostility to Great Britain overseas that Bismarck hoped to build up friendship with France....

By the end of 1855 Bismarck's new policy had laid the foundation of the German Colonial Empire, for by then she had secured her position in the Cameroons and in New Guinea as well as in South-West Africa together with a foothold in East Africa. Where the British Colonial Empire had been founded largely by the private enterprise of the chartered companies, Germany's was created through the impetus of a deliberate policy of state. If that policy met a weak and dilatory response in London, that was due to misunderstanding of its aim and not to unfriendliness. For it was generally accepted that it was right and just that Germany should have her "place in the Sun." Owing to earlier indifference and her late start, her African territories compared unfavourably with those of France or of the Belgians in the Congo Basin, or of the British. But, judged by her subsequent policy, her interest in colonial expansion remained very secondary to her interests in Europe. By 1914 the total number of German colonial settlers was no more than 23,000. While the number of European emigrants is in itself no criterion of the quality of colonial government, these trifling numbers are at least an indication that colonies did not serve as an outlet for surplus population in Germany.

While Germany was acquiring a Colonial Empire in Africa and the Pacific, France, assured of German goodwill, extended her empire chiefly in North and West Africa but also by the acquisition of Madagascar, a convenient stepping-stone to Indo-China, between 1883 and 1885, and after a protracted struggle in Tonkin and Annam. It was the losses and set-backs in Tonkin that brought about the fall of the second [Jules] Ferry Ministry, and with it the end of an active imperialist policy leaning on German goodwill....

The years 1885–89 witnessed the height of the scramble for Africa. But unlike the preceding years they were marked by a revival of Anglo-German co-operation under the aegis of Bismarck and Salisbury. If Bismarck, in laying the foundations of a German Colonial Empire, had not effected a reconciliation with France, he had at least succeeded in his other objectives. France and Italy were estranged over Tunis and Italy was compelled to seek alliance with the Central Powers: England and France were divided by Egypt; and England, partly because of her concern for the security of the Nile Valley, which was the cardinal consideration in determining her colonial policy in Africa, and partly because of the advance of Russia to the Afghan frontier, was also impelled towards more friendly relations with the Central Powers. This had two consequences. The first was the Mediterranean Agreement of 1887 by which England reached an understanding first with Italy later extended to Austria, to preserve the *status quo* in the Mediterranean. Highly satisfying to Bismarck, under whose auspices it was negotiated, the agreement brought England, even if loosely, into the orbit of the Triple Alliance Powers. The other consequence was to be found in the general Anglo-

German colonial settlement in Africa, concluded in 1890 after Bismarck's fall, and made possible by the cession of Heligoland. In the first instance it was hoped by the Germans that South-West Africa might be surrendered for Heligoland. Count Herbert Bismarck, very unfavorably impressed by a visit to South-West Africa, sponsored this proposal. "I think," he wrote on 27th March 1889, "the deal would be very advantageous to us and enormously popular in Germany. Our South-West African Company is stagnant, bankrupt and hopeless. ... In the colonial area we have not in fact a single soul who would qualify as a German citizen." But the negotiations proceeded slowly, largely because Bismarck was once more concerned with the possibility of negotiating a wider agreement with England which would carry European commitments, and partly because he felt it was the course of prudence to go slow lest it might be suspected in London how much importance Germany attached to an island which commanded the entrance to the Kiel Canal, then being built. When agreement was finally reached, the *quid pro quo* for England was not in South-West but mainly in East Africa. The Sultanate of Zanzibar became a British Protectorate and German penetration in East Africa was barred by the delineation of the boundaries of British East Africa....

If German support for French imperial ambitions was an experiment which was tried, failed and abandoned, there was a remarkable consistency about Germany's attitude to Russian expansion in Asia. It was something to be encouraged. About that there were no doubts. It had almost everything to recommend it. It would distract Russia's attention from Europe, thereby lessening the risk of an Austro-Russian conflict in the Balkans; it would keep Russian forces harmlessly occupied; it would, above all, keep alive Anglo-Russian tension by playing on English fears of a Russian invasion of India. "Germany," Bismarck advised his Emperor, "has no interest in preventing Russia if she looks for the occupation which is necessary for her army in Asia rather than Europe. If the Russian Army is unoccupied it becomes a danger to the internal security of the Empire and the dynasty, and if occupation fails in Asia it must necessarily be sought on the Western front.... It is therefore an aim of German policy to-day to bring about hostile rather than too intimate relations between Russia and England."...

In 1889, at the time of transition between the old order of the wild Tartar Khanates and the newer rule of Russia, George Curzon visited Central Asia, conscious that this was the moment when the era of "The Thousand and One Nights" with its strange mixture of savagery and splendour, of coma and excitement, was fast fading, before "the rude shock and unfeeling Philistinism of nineteenth-century civilization," though still in the cities of Alp Arslan, and Timur and Abdullah Khan were to be seen a stage "upon which is yet being enacted that expiring drama of realistic romance." But the future Viceroy of India, who in his own day was to be so profoundly concerned with the building up of the Indian Empire into a continental power capable of withstanding a Russian attack from the north, frankly recognized that Russian rule was firmly and fairly established, and loyally accepted by the conquered races. This he attributed to many factors—the ferocious severity of the original blow; the powerlessness of resistance against the tight military grip of Russia, above all the certainty "which a long course of Russian conduct has reasonably inspired that she will never retreat." The last was the fundamental factor. Tsarist or Communist, the Russian Empire does not retreat in Asia.... When the British Empire in India passed away, the Central Asian Republics of the Soviet Union were only at the dawn of their material development. It is that which in the long run will make Russian expansion in Asia of at least equal significance to the contemporary colonization of Africa by the powers of Western Europe....

It was in January 1895 that President [Paul] Kruger, as the guest of the German Club in Pretoria on the Kaiser's birthday, spoke of Germany as "a grown-up power that would stop England from kicking the child Republic." On instructions from London the British Ambassador protested against the German encouragement of Boer hostility to Britain, of which Kruger's speech was regarded as a provocative expression. The Kaiser later maintained that the Ambassador had gone so far as to mention the "astounding word, 'war.' " "For a few square miles full of niggers and palm trees England had threatened her one true friend, the German Emperor, grandson of Her Majesty the Queen of Great Britain and Ireland, with war!" According to his own highly coloured narrative the Kaiser retorted with the "clear warning" that England could only escape from existing isolation "by a frank and outspoken attitude either for or against the Triple Alliance." As things were England's attitude, her policy "of selfishness and bullying" were forcing Germany to make "common cause with France and Russia, each of whom had about a million men ready to pour in over my frontier...." Into this atmosphere of artificial tension came with explosive effect the news of the Jameson Raid. Ill-judged, ill-considered, wholly indefensible, even in its limited Anglo-South African context, it played straight into the hands of the most dangerous forces at work in Germany. The Kaiser responded with a telegram to President Kruger, dated 3rd January 1896. "I express my sincere congratulations that, supported by your people, without appealing for the help of friendly Powers, you have succeeded by your own energetic action against armed bands which invaded your country as disturbers of the peace, and have thus been enabled to restore peace and safeguard the independence of the country against attacks from the outside." If the telegram was designed to embody every phrase best calculated to inflame sentiment in a country whose first reaction to the news of the Raid was one of profound misgiving, it could not have been better drafted. At once opinion hardened against the Boer Republics. President Kruger was no longer felt to be the much wronged defender of his people's rights, but a collaborator with the Kaiser challenging British rule in South Africa. Self-respect was restored and internal divisions papered over.

To send a telegram was one thing; to intervene effectively in South Africa was another. Germany had no fleet. What course was open to her? Holstein[4] supplied the answer. The Triple Alliance and the Dual Alliance should forget their rivalry and co-operate against Britain. There was a wide field for common action and many colonial ambitions that could be achieved in concert. France should receive the Congo Free State, Germany further concessions in China,

[4] Baron von Holstein was a high official in the German Foreign Office and a formulator of Germany's anti-British policy—Ed.

Russia, Korea; Italy would become the Protector of Abyssinia. This superficially was a tempting prospect for one and all. But behind it there were subtle reservations, soon suspected. The ultimate German intention was not the final estrangement of Britain but a practical demonstration of the dangers of isolation and of the need to co-operate with the Triple Alliance. That was why there was no mention of Egypt. In the sequel it was in Paris that this grandiose plan received its death sentence. It was Egypt alone by which France might have been momentarily deluded into a dangerous partnership and Egypt was not on offer. Moreover, the immediate background to this continental League lay in the Transvaal, and the Transvaal was of no interest to France, however much its people might sympathize with the Boer cause. . . .

Holstein's project of European Alliance was stillborn, and it is interesting to notice that when the South African War broke out in 1899, Germany's policy was very different. In 1900 it was Russia who proposed mediation and Germany who declined it, the Kaiser improving the occasion by informing the Queen and the Prince of Wales of his refusal. The Prince paid ironic tribute to this gesture thanking the Kaiser in March 1900—"You have no idea, my dear William, how all of us in England appreciate the loyal friendship you manifest towards us on every occasion." But if the political response was more judicious the lesson deduced in Berlin from the Raid and the South African War was always the same—sea power is the condition of world power. That was the most significant legacy of the Jameson Raid and the South African War to Europe. . . .

Though on more than one occasion colonial rivalries brought the Great Powers within sight of war, it is not for that reason to be concluded that colonial rivalry was a fundamental cause of war. On the contrary the colonial policies of the Continental states were formulated in the light of the European balance of power and designed to serve European ends. When they no longer served those ends the colonial scene slips unobtrusively into the background. From 1900 onwards there were no important colonial disputes between Germany and England because of the preoccupation of the Powers in the Far East between 1900–1904; and after 1904 because the Anglo-French Entente had removed the possibility of attaining the political ends which German colonial policy in the 'eighties had been designed to promote. But if in general the colonial policies of the Powers were subordinate to their European interests, that is not to say that colonial rivalry had little effect on the course of European history, but merely that its consequences were indirect. Of them, two were of outstanding importance. The first was the conviction created in Germany that a powerful navy was an indispensable means to world power; the second was the decline in international morality fostered by the corroding impact of an unscrupulous scramble for, and subsequent exploitation of, overseas territories.

SARDAR KAVALAM MADHAVA PANIKKAR (1895–1963) was one of India's most distinguished historians. He was educated at Madras University, Oxford, and the Middle Temple; was editor of the influential *Hindustan Times;* and was a professor at Aligarh Muslim University. His varied background, combined with his practical knowledge of diplomacy gained from serving as Indian ambassador to China, 1948–1952, Egypt, 1952–1953, and France, 1956–1959, gave him a rare ability to interpret both Eastern and Western customs. He was an Indian nationalist, but one who was quite prepared to see the benefits as well as the harm from British overrule. In the following selection he wrote of imperialism from an Eastern and cultural point of view.*

An Eastern View of British Imperialism

The 450 years which began with the arrival of Vasco da Gama in Calicut (in 1498), and ended with the withdrawal of British forces from India in 1947 and of the European navies from China in 1949, constitute a clearly marked epoch of history. It may have passed through many stages, undergone different developments, appeared in different periods under different leadership, but as a whole it had certain well-marked characteristics which differentiated it as a separate epoch in history. Its motivations underwent changes; one major strand in the original idea, that of a crusade against Islam and a strategic outflanking of Muslim power, disappeared after the menace to Western Europe from the growth of Islamic imperialism ended with the Battle of Lepanto. The original desire for the monopoly of the spice trade changed in a hundred years to the import into Europe of textiles, tea and other goods, which again changed after the Industrial Revolution in Britain into an urge to find markets for European manufactured goods and finally for investment of capital. Originally confined to trade, European interests became in the nineteenth century predominantly political over many years. The leadership of European peoples in this period also underwent change. From Portugal the supremacy in trade was wrested by the Dutch. In the middle of the eighteenth century Britain and France con-

* From K. M. Panikkar, *Asia and Western Dominance: A Survey of the Vasco Da Gama Epoch of Asian History, 1498–1945* (new ed.; London, 1959). Reprinted by permission of George Allen and Unwin Ltd.

tested for it for a short time. Since then, the authority of Britain was never seriously challenged till the beginning of the Second World War.

In spite of these changes and developments, it is none the less true that the da Gama epoch presents a singular unity in its fundamental aspects. These may be briefly stated as the dominance of maritime power over the land masses of Asia; the imposition of a commercial economy over communities whose economic life in the past had been based not on international trade, but mainly on agricultural production and internal trade; and thirdly the domination of the peoples of Europe, who held the mastery of the seas, over the affairs of Asia. It was an age of maritime power, of authority based on the control of the seas. Till the beginning of the present century, for a period of 400 years from the time of Vasco da Gama, sea power, capable of deciding Oceanic policies, did not exist outside the Atlantic. The control of the Atlantic thus meant the mastery of the Indian Ocean and ultimately of the Pacific. During the first hundred years the Iberian powers had the mastery of the Atlantic, but from the time of dispersal of Philip of Spain's Armada, that supremacy began gradually to diminish and was inherited by other European Powers. The essential feature, that of the control of the Asian seas, remained....

...European expansion towards the East began as a crusade. It was the beginning of one of the great Crusades, the Eighth Crusade we might call it. The leadership of this movement was inherited from Henry the Navigator, not only by Manoel the Fortunate and Joao III, but by Affonso Albuquerque and other leaders of Portuguese expansion who looked upon themselves as genuine crusaders. Every blow struck at the Moor was, in their view, a victory for Christendom. The attack on the spice trade, as Albuquerque clearly explained to his soldiers at Malacca, was an attack on the financial prosperity of the Muslim nations, an aspect of economic warfare the significance of which both the Muslim Powers and Portugal fully realized. This crusading attitude had certain significant results. With the non-Muslim peoples and rulers of Asia, the relations of the Portuguese were not, generally speaking, unfriendly.

The crusading and anti-Muslim aspect of European expansion in Asia ceased to be a major factor by the beginning of the seventeenth century, owing to two important reasons. In the first place, the Protestant movement had broken up the unity of Christendom, and the religious fanaticism which was previously directed against Islam was now turned to civil war in Europe. The Wars of Religion, which devastated Europe for over a century and ended only with the Treaty of Westphalia, tended to obliterate the memory of the Muslim menace, which ceased from then to be a "primary motive" in European history. The second was the Battle of Lepanto where Don Juan of Austria, or Christian Europe, destroyed the naval power of the Turks....

The crusading spirit was replaced, so far as the [Roman] Catholic countries were concerned, by a spirit of evangelization. The upsurge in the Catholic religion, of which the most characteristic expression was the Society of Jesus, saw in the East great prospects of evangelization. The Portuguese monarchy was deeply influenced by this, and we have from this time a new urge which sent Jesuit fathers to the courts of the Grand Mogul, the Chinese Emperor and the Shogun. This urge weakened a little with the arrival of the Dutch and the English in Asian waters, for till the beginning of the nineteenth century Protestant churches did not feel the call of converting the heathen and entering seriously into the mission field. But in the nineteenth century, and up to the First European War, evangelization again becomes a major urge in European relations with Asia. It may indeed be said that the most serious, persistent and planned effort of European nations in the nineteenth century was their missionary activities in India and China, where a large-scale attempt was made to effect a mental and spiritual conquest as supplementing the political authority already enjoyed by Europe. Though the results were disappointing in the extreme from the missionary point of view, this assult on the spiritual foundations of Asian countries has had far-reaching consequences in the religious and social reorganization of the peoples. . . . Indeed, it might be appropriately said that while political aggrandisement was the work of governments and groups, and commerce the interest of organized capital, mission work was the effort of the people of the West to bring home to the masses of Asia their view of the values of life.

Religion, however, was only one aspect of European expansion. Even with the Portuguese, who in the beginning equated the establishment of a monopoly in spice trade with religion, trade soon overshadowed the religious aspect of their work. With the arrival of the Protestant Powers trade became for a time the only consideration. There was little contact outside commercial relations. . . . In the trading period, 1610–1758, Europe influenced Asia but little.

In the period of conquest (1750–1857), however, the situation began to change. Asian leaders began to feel that the strangers had become a menace and had to be taken seriously. It is not surprising that the first serious interest that the Asian leaders began to show was in cannon-making, army organization and military equipment. But apart from this justifiable curiosity in respect of military matters shown by a few people in power, there were others who were interested in the intellectual and spiritual strength of the European nations. . . .

The most significant single factor which changed the intellectual relationship of Europe and Asia was the French Revolution. . . . Negroes in Haiti, Tipoo in Mysore, Dutch radicals in Indonesia, all felt the ripples of this movement. . . . Wellesley's[1] aggressive policy leading to the conquest and annexation of large areas of India was one of its indirect consequences, for it was the fear of the revolutionary French that provided the main motive of his policy of conquest. But it is not in this sense that the doctrines of the French Revolution—"liberty, equality and fraternity"—came to have a pervading influence on Asia. As a revolution the developments in France had but little immediate influence on the Asian people. In the period that followed the Napoleonic experiment, the doctrines of the Revolution had become the common inheritance of European liberalism. Modified and made respectable by the reformers in the period immediately following the Napoleonic era, they became the mental background of European statesmen. Education could no longer be neglected in the possessions of European nations. Codes of modern law had to be provided. . . . Slowly a liberal tradition penetrated the policies of European nations.

Not only did the French revolutionary

[1] The Marquis of Wellesley (then Lord Mornington) came to India as governor general in 1798 and worked to make the East India Company supreme in the subcontinent. He is not to be confused with Arthur Wellesley, later Duke of Wellington, who destroyed Maratha military power at Assaye in 1803—Ed.

doctrines become in due course an influence on European thought in relation to the East, but they provided the Asian peoples with their first political ideology. Indian writings of the first period of nationalism hark back to the principles of this school. Ram Mohan Roy[2] and his followers, petitioning for the abolition of *Suttee,* for education in English, for greater freedom for women, though they quote from Hindu scriptures in justification of their reforms, are really thinking in terms of Rousseau, watered down to meet Indian conditions. European inspirations of the Asian reform movements of the first half of the nineteenth century cannot be denied.

The nineteenth century witnessed the apogee of capitalism in Europe.... It is the riches of Asian trade (and American) flowing to Europe that enabled the great industrial revolution to take place in England. But with the establishment of capitalism as the dominant economic structure of the colonizing nations, an immense and far-reaching change took place in the relations of the West with Asia. In the eighteenth century, conquest was for the purpose of trade. In the area you conquered, you excluded other nations, bought at the cheapest price, organized production by forced labour to suit your requirements, and transferred the profits to the mother country. In the nineteenth century conquest was not for trade but for investment. Tea plantations and railway construction became major interests in Britain's connection with India. Vast sums were invested in India for building railways. "Of the loans for Indian Railways," says an English writer, "about one-third went to pay the home charges in London, something under one-third was spent on wages and administrative expenses, largely paid to English engineers, and something over one-third on British rails and engines and in paying British ships to bring them to India."[3]

The third phase of European relations with Asia, which begins with the middle of the nineteenth century, is the period of imperialism in the true sense of the word. The transformation is completed earliest in India, which provides the pattern for the rest, for the Dutch in Indonesia, for the French in Indo-China, for all the nations in respect of China. The imperialist relationship, involving large-scale capital investment, had the result of importing into Asia advanced technical skills and scientific knowledge. Railway construction, which was the main field of capital investment, required the importation of engineers. Rivers had to be spanned, tunnels had to be built, and the lines, once constructed, had to be maintained. Imported technical skill, except at the highest levels, became too costly, and as a result engineering colleges and schools became unavoidable. The spread of technical knowledge in the East, of which this is merely an example, was a necessary result of capital investment. It was not possible to keep Asian nationals out of this knowledge, for returns on capital depended on finding technical skill locally. In regard to industry also, a similar movement became noticeable. European industries established in Calcutta, Bombay and Shanghai had to depend, at least in their lower levels, on locally trained personnel. With the advancement of knowledge among local populations it became impossible to prevent Asian capital from encroaching on European industrial monopolies. In

[2] Ram Mohan Roy, 1772–1833, "the father of the Hindu Reformation," was much influenced by the thinkers of the European Enlightenment—Ed.

[3] Quoted in Charles E. Carrington, *The British Overseas: Exploits of a Nation of Shopkeepers* (Cambridge, Eng., 1950), p. 479. (Expanded note—Ed.)

India, cotton mills began to spring up in Bombay and Ahmedabad. In Shanghai, which had become practically a European city, Chinese industrialists found no difficulty in setting up factories in imitation of European models. Railway construction in China, which was a subject of furious international competition, when it was first taken up, soon became an activity of the Chinese Government. Thus, in its primary aspect, imperialism as an export of capital carried into Asia the seeds of its own destruction.

In its second aspect, that is territorial expansion for providing areas for exploitation, European imperialism in the nineteenth century, under the humanitarian impulses of the liberal movement, embarked on a policy of education, welfare schemes and even political training. Direct administration of vast populations naturally created new interests. The administrative authorities had no direct connection with or interest in trade, the officers being, at least according to English tradition, recruited from the middle classes with public school training. So in India, and to some extent in Indonesia, a contradiction developed within the structure of imperialism in which the administrative authorities were inclined to emphasize the welfare aspect of their work, while the commercial interests still considered the territories as areas for exploitation. . . . In fact political authority, combined with the humanitarian ideals of the era of peace, brought a sense of responsibility towards "the backward peoples." No danger to the supremacy of Europe was suspected as being inherent in this development, for even at the end of the nineteenth century the Europeans —even the most progressive among them —were convinced that their superiority was divinely ordained and was safe at least for centuries to come. The idea that the Chinese, weak, immobilized and without industrial potential, could stand up and fight the European within a measurable time, or that Indians could compete with the British in trade or industry, or that the hundreds of Indonesian islands could be united in opposition to the Dutch, would have sounded ludicrous to a European in the Augustan age of imperialism. Therefore the humanitarian ideal of educating the Asian people and of encouraging them to develop at least those skills which were necessary for the more effective discharge of the white man's mission, was pursued without any sense of fear.

Also, the complexities of direct administration of vast areas like India and Indonesia made it necessary to develop a large body of indigenous administrative personnel. In the period of trade there was no such necessity. In the period of imperialism this was unavoidable.

The apparatus of modern States, run largely by local talent, had to be built up, providing the Asian peoples both with administrative training and with knowledge and understanding of the mechanism of modern government. This is particularly important, for one of the main differences between the earlier periods of history and the political systems that developed in the nineteenth and twentieth centuries lay in the vast administrative systems which touched every aspect of life which the State organizations of the nineteenth and twentieth centuries represented. . . .

The Asian State-systems, though essentially bureaucratic and therefore "administrative" and not political, were, however, limited to land administration and defence. The Administrative system which the Crown developed in India and which every colonial administration felt compelled to develop in its territory, not only provided the first conception of the modern State to the Asian mind, but equipped it with the mechanism necessary to realize it in time. . . .

The third aspect of territorial expansion—of the era of imperialism—was the popular sentiment of responsibility for "moral wellbeing" which found its most characteristic expression in the missionary work. The conscience of the people, especially of the Protestant countries, was aroused by the fact that in the areas directly governed by them or under their influence hundreds of millions lived and died without the chance of salvation. . . . Though the results of their religious activities were negligible and often led only to reactions which they least expected, their interest in the life and wellbeing of the common people, and their efforts to break down the barrier of race, had the benefit of bringing the West nearer to Asia. Also, their educational and medical work in the interior of India, China and Burma had far-reaching consequences.

It is necessary to emphasize that the contact between the peoples of the East with Europeans began really only in the era of imperialism. In the 300 and odd years that preceded it (from 1498 to 1858) this contact was limited, even in India, to narrow circles, and had not penetrated even into the ruling classes. With direct administration, development of educational systems, exploitation instead of trade, the contact gradually extended to different levels. Slowly Asian youths began to find their way to European seats of learning. . . . The first impulse which took young Indians across the seas was not to probe the mysteries of European life, but the more material consideration of a chance to compete in the Civil Service examination. But soon this movement assumed immense proportions, and a large proportion of the students who went to Europe were dedicated to the study of such subjects as engineering, medicine, forestry, geology and chemistry apart, of course, from law and social sciences. A similar movement took large numbers of Indo-Chinese students to Paris and Indonesians to Leyden. The prestige of German technical advances attracted a growing number to the universities of the Reich.

The essential point for our purpose is that in every one of the countries of Asia, the leadership in the movement which ultimately displaced European supremacy belonged to those who had been trained by the West under the aegis of imperialism. Not only Mahatma Gandhi and Jawaharlal Nehru, but the founders of the Indian National Congress and the successive generations of Congress leaders were trained in the West. In Japan, it was the group of explorers sent to the West by the Shogunate that led the movement for the reorganization of the State. In China, though the deposition of the Manchus was not the work of Western-educated people, the building up of the revolutionary movement that followed was led by men of Western training. In Indonesia, Indo-China, Burma and Ceylon it is the men and women educated in the West—the "Wogs" (Westernized Oriental gentlemen) as the European contemptuously called them—that provided the leadership. . . .

Nationalism in indubitably the most significant development in Asian countries during the last hundred years of European contact. It is often stated by European writers that Asian peoples had no sense of nationalism or even of nationality till they came into contact with European peoples. This criticism ignores the fact that in Europe itself the doctrine of nationalism developed mainly as a result of resistance to Napoleonic aggrandisement. No doubt England and

France had deep-seated patriotic feeling, but in the multi-national Empire of the Habsburgs, which included Lombardy as well as portions of Poland, patriotism had to be equated with dynastic loyalty. It is, therefore, not unreasonable to emphasize that the development of nationalism in Asia, as an overriding loyalty to a State embodying a continuous tradition and supposed to represent a single people, was a parallel growth to the same movement in Europe and arose out of similar circumstances, that is, resistance to foreign rule. . . .

This cult of the nation required in many cases a new historical background, for without a common history a nation cannot exist. In many Asian countries, especially India, such a history with a national purpose seemed hardly to exist. India had an undoubted geographical, cultural, social and even religious unity in the sense that all through its history ran the main thread of Hindu religious development. But political history was practically unknown except as myths and legends. From the identification of Sandrocottus as Chandragupta Maurya[4] to the excavations of Mohenjodaro and Harappa,[5] from the deciphering of the inscriptions of Asoka[6] to the comprehensive survey of epigraphic records all over India, the material for the writing of Indian history was provided by the work of European scholars. Even more striking is the case of Indonesia, where a few European scholars, mostly Dutch, reconstructed from inscriptions the history of the great empires of Java and Sumatra which provided Indonesian nationalism with a solid historical basis. In this sense it cannot be denied that European scholars and thinkers, by their labours in the interests of knowledge, enabled India, Ceylon and Indonesia to think in terms of historic community. . . .

It should also be remembered that the European nations in emphasizing their solidarity, their *European-ness* in dealing with Asian countries, inevitably gave rise to a common feeling of Asian-ness. Even in India, where nationals of other European countries enjoyed no political rights, the division was between Europeans and Indians and not between Englishmen and Indians. The exclusive clubs in India were not for Englishmen, but for *Europeans.* Special schools and educational facilities that existed were also for Europeans. In China, where all European countries enjoyed political privileges, the European communities went to great lengths to present a united front. Even when the Franco-German War was being fought in Europe, the pressure of the doctrine of European solidarity against Asians compelled the German Minister to line up behind his French colleagues in the affair of Tientsin. . . . From 1800 to 1914 . . . the Europeans were united against Asia, and this attitude, in its turn, gave birth to a sense of Asianism. . . .

There is a view generally held by many European writers that the changes brought about in Asia by the contact with Europe are superficial and will, with the disappearance of European political authority, cease to count as time goes on. . . . This point of view would seem to be based on a superficial reading of history. . . .

The first and perhaps the most abiding influence is in the sphere of law. In all

[4] Chandragupta, c. 321–c. 297 B.C., founded the Maurya Dynasty by being the first to unite northern India—Ed.

[5] See A. L. Basham, *The Wonder that was India* (London, 1954), on these ancient cities —Ed.

[6] Asoka, c. 274–c. 236 B.C., extended his holdings by further conquest and left edicts engraved in Prakrit on rocks and pillars throughout his empire—Ed.

Asian countries the legal systems have been fundamentally changed and reorganized according to the post-revolutionary conceptions of nineteenth-century Europe. The first country in which this change was introduced was India where, under the influence of Thomas Babington Macaulay, new legal principles were systematically introduced and applied. I may quote here what I have written elsewhere in this connection: "The legal system under which India has lived for a hundred years and within whose steel frame her social, political and economic development has taken place, is the work of Macaulay. . . . The establishment of the great principle of equality of all before law in a country where under the Hindu doctrines a Brahmin could not be punished on the evidence of a Sudra, and even punishments varied according to caste, and where, according to Muslim law, testimony could not be accepted against a Muslim was itself a legal revolution of the first importance. . . ."[7] The transformation brought about by the new legal doctrines of the West is a permanent one and is likely to outlast the more spectacular changes in many other fields. . . .

It is not possible to speak with the same certainty about the political and social structures brought about as a result of the conflict with Europe. The forms of Government, the nature of political rights, democracy in its widest sense, local and municipal administrations—these may all disappear, change their character or survive only in attenuated and unrecognizable forms in certain areas. And yet at the present time they constitute the most spectacular change in Asia. No country in the East is now governed under a system of "Oriental Despotism." Even Japan, where the divinely descended Emperor reigns in an unbroken line of succession, is now clothed will all the paraphernalia of a democratic constitution. In fact, the norm of Government in the East has become a republic. While in Europe there are still six [now five] sovereigns and a Grand Duchess, in non-Islamic Asia there are only three monarchies (Japan, Siam and Nepal), while all the nations which acquired their independence or threw off foreign domination have been proclaimed republics. . . .

The growth of great cities, themselves centres of political and economic dynamism, is a result of European contacts, the immense significance of which has not been fully appreciated. . . . The towns and cities in India, when they were not great capitals, were merely great centres of population, sometimes important from the point of view of trade, often from the point of view of religious sanctity. They did not involve any civic tradition. The same was the case in China.

The new cities, which grew up as a result of European contacts, Bombay, Calcutta and Madras, Shanghai, Tientsin, Singapore, Colombo, Jakarta, etc., represent a new principle: the organization of the city as an independent unit. In Madras, Calcutta and Bombay we have the full paraphernalia of European city life, with sheriffs, mayors, corporations and aldermen. From this point of view, the organization of the Municipal Committee of Shanghai by the British merchants, and its phenomenal growth during a period of seventy years, may represent a greater and more far-reaching change than the control exercised by the foreigners on the imperial court.

It is the city that has created the wealthy middle classes in India, China and other Asian countries. The emergence of the middle classes both as leaders

[7] Panikkar, *A Survey of Indian History* (3d ed.; Bombay, 1956), p. 257. (Expanded note—Ed.)

in political and economic life and as reservoirs of essential scientific skills, has been in the main the outcome of the new life in the cities. The possibility of the great cities surviving as centres of civilization, even if regression sets in elsewhere inside the countries of Asia much in the same way as in medieval Europe, cannot be overlooked, and if that happens the credit for the survival of the new life in the great cities will certainly belong to Europe.

Another point, one which arises directly out of Europe's long domination over Asia, is the integration of vast territories into great nation States of a kind unknown in the previous history of Asia. India, for instance, all through her long history, had never been welded together into a single State as she is now....

...For the first time in history, India has been integrated into a single State living under the same constitution and subject to the same laws. Unquestionably this was the result of a hundred years of British administration which imposed a unity on the peoples of India, both by the machinery of Government which it created and by the forces of resistance to which it gave rise. Even more striking is the case of Indonesia. In the past these islands had never been united into a single political organization. Nor was it ever the dream of the great Empires of Java and Sumatra to weld the whole archipelago into one State. The Sailendra monarchs of Srivijaya, in the greatness of their maritime strength, never dreamed of claiming suzerainty even over the whole of Java, let alone Borneo, Moluccas and the innumerable islands of the Sundas. When the Europeans arrived in the islands there was no feeling of Indonesian unity. The present unity of the islands is therefore the result of the 450 years of contact with Europe, and the political and economic ties created by the Dutch....

Philosophy and religious thinking, however much they may influence the people in general, are the special interests of the intellectuals. But not so the language, and it is here that the influence of Europe has been most noticeable. From the great literatures of China, India and Japan to the minor languages spoken only by a few million people, everywhere the influence of the West overshadows past traditions. The literary Revolution in China (1918–21) will perhaps be considered in future a more significant event than the many revolutions that country has undergone in this century. Today in China the forms of writing which are followed show little or no influence of the classics, and are modelled upon the literature of the West. The Chinese novel today does not follow the *Dream of the Red Chamber*,[8] or the story of the three kingdoms, but is created in the mould of Tolstoy, Turgenev, Romain Rolland, Thomas Mann and Maxim Gorky.... During the past twenty years in China all creative writing has been dominated by Europe.

The instance of India is even more significant. In the great languages of India there was at first no revolutionary break with the past. In fact, till about 1914, though the Western forms of writing had taken deep root in the languages, and novels, short stories and dramas were popular and had gained a hold on the public mind, it was the classical tradition that was still dominant. . . . During the last thirty years, however, the literatures of the great Indian languages have undergone a revolutionary change. They are no longer concerned with the refinements of classical style. They bor-

[8] Written in the eighteenth century by Tsao Hsueh-chin and Kao Ngoh—Ed.

row freely from all the literatures of the West....[9]

It should however, be emphasized that the increasing acceptance of new ideas... does not involve a break in the continuity of the great Asian civilizations. The Chinese, Indian and other civilizations, though modified by new ideas and enriched by new experience, continue even in an increasing degree to emphasize their special characteristics. In South and South-east Asia and in Japan this, to a large extent, is the result of the strength of the reorganized religion. The failure of the Christian attack on Hinduism, Buddhism and, of course, Islam, left them stronger and more vigorous as a result of the adjustments they were called upon to effect. In China, where the missionary activity achieved the limited success of breaking down religious traditions, the attachment to national civilization is still profound and is strengthened by racial and psychological characteristics which cannot be easily changed. Thus, though the influence of Europe and the penetration of new ideas have introduced vast changes in Asia, and may lead to even greater changes, Asian civilizations will continue to develop their marked individuality and remain spiritually and intellectually separate from Christian Europe....

The new Asian States... can no longer revert to a policy of isolation or pretend ignorance of the existence of other countries. China, India and Indonesia—apart, of course, from Japan—have therefore no mean roles to fill in the politics of the present-day world. That arises directly from the transformation caused by Europe's former Empires over the East.

The effects of Asian contacts on Europe, though considerably less, cannot be considered insignificant. The growth of capitalism in the seventeenth, eighteenth and nineteenth centuries, in itself a profound and revolutionary change, is intimately connected with the expansion of European trade and business into Asia. The political development of the leading Western European nations during this period was also related to their exploitation of their Asian possessions and the wealth they derived from the trade with and government of their Eastern dependencies. The material life, as reflected in clothing, food, beverages, etc., also bears permanent marks of their Eastern contacts.... The influence of Chinese literature and of Indian philosophical thought, to mention only two trends which have become important in recent years, cannot be evaluated for many years to come. Yet it is true... that most modern poets in Europe have in some measure been influenced by the literature of China. Equally the number of translations of the *Bhagavad Gita* and the *Upanishads,* which have been appearing every year, meant not for Orientalists and scholars but for the educated public, and the revival of interest in the religious experience of India, are sufficient to prove that a penetration of European thought by Oriental influences is now taking place which future historians may consider to be of some significance.

Also, archaeology has seriously affected the faith which was so firmly held in the past that everything of value developed on the shores of the Mediterranean. The past of the Great Asian peoples has gradually come to be considered as part of the general heritage of civilized man, and this may in time lead to a breakdown of the narrow Europeanism, which considered everything outside the experience of the West of secondary importance.

[9] Notably R. K. Narayan, K. S. Venkataramani, M. R. Anand, and Kamala Markhandaya—Ed.

Key questions remain unresolved. What is needed is a careful restatement of the problem, bringing together the many interpretations of imperialism. Recently three historians, RONALD ROBINSON (1920–) of St. John's College, Cambridge; JOHN GALLAGHER (1919–) of Trinity College, Cambridge; and ALICE DENNY (Mrs. Robinson, 1926–), an American-trained researcher, implicitly posed several such omnibus questions. All three are well acquainted with Africa, in particular, and Dr. Robinson is a veteran of the African Studies branch of the Colonial Office. The conclusion to their book, *Africa and the Victorians*, is in fact an invitation to begin anew our study of British imperialism.*

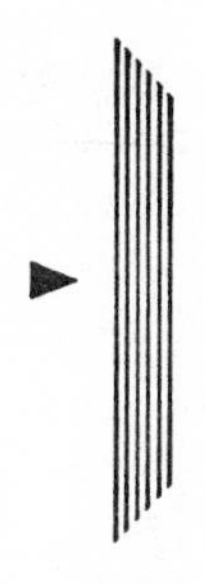

A Synthesis of Views and a Challenge for the Future

At the centre of late-Victorian imperialism in Africa lies an apparent paradox. The main streams of British trade, investment and migration continued to leave tropical Africa practically untouched; and yet it was tropical Africa that was now bundled into the empire. There is a striking discrepancy of direction here between the economic and imperial arms. The flag was not following trade and capital; nor were trade and capital as yet following the flag. The late-Victorians seemed to be concentrating their imperial effort in the continent of least importance to their prosperity.

What were the causes and incentives? Which of them were merely contributory and which decisive? The question of the motives for African empire may be opened afresh. There are several well-known elements in the problem. Perhaps the late-Victorians were more enthusiastic imperialists than their fathers. Possibly business men were driven to bring the unopened continent into production and so relieve surfeit and depression. . . . Or it may be that heightened rivalries between the Powers in Europe made them seek relief in Africa from their tensions nearer home. For any or all of these reasons, the forces of imperialism in Britain and in Europe may have intensified dramatically in the last quarter of the century and caught up all Africa as they did so.

* From Ronald Robinson, John Gallagher, with Alice Denny, *Africa and the Victorians: The Climax of Imperialism in the Dark Continent* (New York, 1961). By permission of St. Martin's Press and the authors.

But in the British case at least, there are other possible elements which have sometimes been neglected. It cannot be taken for granted that positive impulses from European society or the European economy were alone in starting up imperial rivalries. The collapse of African governments under the strain of previous Western influences may have played a part, even a predominant part in the process. The British advances may have been the culmination of the destructive workings of earlier exercises of informal empire over the coastal *régimes.* Hence crises in Africa, no less than imperial ambitions and international rivalries in Europe, have to be taken into account. Allowance has also to be made for the diversity of interest and circumstance in the different regions of Africa. It seems unlikely that the motives in regions as dissimilar as Egypt, the Niger and south Africa can be fitted easily into a single, simple formula of "imperialism."

Another factor must be included. Victorian expansion by the Eighteen eighties had long historical roots and world-wide ramifications. Its manifold workings tended sometimes to build up, and sometimes to break down the societies drawn under its influence. While in some countries, British agencies helped to create vortices of disorder and nationalist reaction, in others they helped local communities to grow until they became expansive in their own right. In these ways the processes of expansion were soon receding out of metropolitan control. Some satellites tended to break up; others were beginning to throw off galaxies of their own. It is not unlikely that both these tendencies helped to drag British ministries into African empire. Lastly, it is quite possible that they did not acquire a new empire for its intrinsic value, but because Africa's relationship to their total strategy in Europe, the Mediterranean, or the East had altered.

The elements in the problem might seem so numerous and disparate as to make it insoluble. Some unified field of study has to be found where all possible incentives to African empire may be assembled without becoming indistinguishable in their several effects. Historically, only the government in London registered and balanced all the contingencies making for British expansion in Africa. In following the occasions and motives, all roads lead ineluctably to Downing Street. The files and red boxes which passed between ministers and officials at the time contain the problem in its contemporary proportions.

The collective mind of government assembled and weighed all the factors making for and against advances. Party leaders and Whips anxiously consulted the tone of the Commons and the trend of the by-elections. Secretaries for India, the Colonies and Foreign Affairs, along with the Chancellor of the Exchequer and the Service ministers, gauged the pressures: the condition of domestic and European politics, the state of the economy, the expansive demands from India and the white colonies, the risks and crises in Africa and in the whole world. Furnished with intelligences from distant ambassadors, governors and consuls, they took the rival theses of their departments to the Cabinet; and there, the Prime Minister and his colleagues argued out the differences and balanced the considerations of profit and power.

A first task in analysing the late-Victorians' share in the partition is to understand the motives of the ministers who directed it, and the study of official thinking is indispensable to this. Policy-making was a flow of deliberation and argument, of calculation and meditation between differing impulses. Secondly, it was a reading of the long-run national interest which stayed much the same from ministry to ministry, regardless of the ideological stock in trade of the Party in power. Ministers in their private calculations used a complex political arithmetic to decide whether to advance or not. Their thinking included analogues for the expansive pressures coming from business enterprise and Home politics, from foreign rivals and British agents on the spot.

By trying to reconstruct the calculations behind the higher decisions, the interplay of these elements as they worked at different levels may begin to emerge. The study of government's own reasoning is the obvious yardstick for measuring the urgency of incentives and contingencies at the point of action. Policy-making, in other words, is the unified historical field in which all the conditions for expansion were brought together.

This is not to say that ministers and their advisers were fully aware of the forces at work, or that they knew to a nicety where they were going. Neither is it to say that they were in control of the process of expansion and could start and stop it at will. Again, their recorded arguments for this course or for that did not always bring out fully their unconscious assumptions. What is more, there are many things too well understood between colleagues to be written down. There is no denying these limitations to the study of policy. But for all its shortcomings, official calculations . . . offer the unique method for making a first approximation to the relative strength of the different drives. . . .

Statesmen did more than respond to pressures and calculate interests; their decisions were not mere mechanical choices of expedients. Judgments and actions in fact were heavily prejudiced by their beliefs about morals and politics, about the duties of government, the ordering of society and international relations. And their attitudes to such questions tended to be specialised and idiosyncratic because they felt that their unique function and responsibility set them apart. If official thinking was in one sense a microcosm of past and present experience of expansion, in another sense, it was consciously above and outside those processes. The aristocrat by right, the official by *expertise,* both felt socially superior and functionally detached from those who pushed trade and built empires. It was their high calling to mediate between jarring and selfish interests and to keep the state from being used as the tool of any of them. As governors, their profession was to take the long and the broad, not the short and narrow view, to reconcile one principle with another in action. . . . Whether a man entered the ruling circle through patronage, which was still usual, or through examination, which was becoming less rare, aristocratic traditions of duty to the whole nation and disdain for its parts persisted, as did the legalism with which they approached their problems. . . .

But the London policy-makers' detachment from their problems overseas was physical as well as professional. In Africa they were usually dealing with countries which they had never seen, with questions apprehended intellectually from reports and recommendations on paper. Their solutions and purposes on the other hand, were charged with the experience and beliefs of the society in which they lived and worked. Inevitably, the official idea and the African reality . . . were worlds apart. Yet in the end it was the idea and the analysis of

African situations in Whitehall, and not the realities in Africa as such which moved Victorian statesmen to act or not to act. The working of their minds is therefore of the utmost importance in establishing the motives of imperialism. Because those who finally decided the issue of African empire were partly insulated from pressures at Home, and remote from reality in Africa, their historical notions, their ideas of international legality and the codes of honour shared by the aristocratic castes of Europe had unusually wide scope in their decisions.

The possibility that official thinking in itself was a cause of late-Victorian imperialism, although once brilliantly suggested by an economist [Schumpeter], has usually been neglected by historians....

To be sure, a variety of different interests in London... pressed for territorial advances and were sometimes used as their agents. In west Africa, the traders called for government protection; in Uganda and Nyasaland, the missionaries and the anti-slavery groups called for annexation; in Egypt, the bondholders asked government to rescue their investments; in south Africa, philanthropists and imperialists called for more government from Whitehall, while British traders and investors were divided about the best way of looking after their interests. Ministers usually listened to their pleas only when it suited their purpose; but commercial and philanthropic agitation seldom decided which territories should be claimed or occupied or when this should be done, although their slogans were frequently used by government in its public justifications.

...For all the different situations in which territory was claimed, and all the different reasons which were given to justify it, one consideration, and one alone entered into all the major decisions. In all regions north of Rhodesia, the broad imperative which decided which territory to reserve and which to renounce, was the safety of the routes to the East. It did not, of course, prompt the claiming of Nyasaland or the lower Niger. Here a reluctant government acted to protect existing fields of trading and missionary enterprise from foreign annexations. In southern Africa the extension of empire seems to have been dictated by a somewhat different imperative. Here the London goverment felt bound as a rule to satisfy the demands for more territory which their self-governing colonials pressed on them. Ministers did this in the hope of conserving imperial influence. Nevertheless, the safety of the routes to India also figured prominently in the decision to uphold British supremacy in south Africa. It was the same imperative which after impelling the occupation of Egypt, prolonged it, and forced Britain to go into east Africa and the Upper Nile, while yielding in most of west Africa.... What decided when and where they would go forward was their traditional conception of world strategy.

Its principles had been distilled from a century and more of accumulated experience, from far-reaching and varied experiments in the uses of power to promote trade and in the uses of trade to promote power. Much of this experience confirmed one precept: that Britain's strength depended upon the possession of India and preponderance in the East, almost as much as it did upon the British Isles. Therefore, her position in the world hung above all upon safe communications between the two. This was a supreme interest of Victorian policy; it set the order of priorities in the Middle East and Asia, no less than in Africa, and when African situations interlocked with it, they engaged the serious and urgent attention of the British government. At the first level of analysis, the decisive motive behind late-Victorian strategy in Africa was to protect the all-important stakes in India and the East....

Hence the question of motive should be formulated afresh. It is no longer the winning of a new empire in Africa which has to be explained. The question is simpler: Why could the late-Victorians after 1880 no longer rely upon influence to protect traditional interests? What forced them in the end into imperial solutions? The answer is to be found first in the nationalist crises in Africa itself, which were the work of intensifying European influences during previous decades; and only secondarily in the interlocking of these crises in Africa with rivalries in Europe. Together the two drove Britain step by step to regain by territorial claims and occupation that security which could no longer be had by influence alone. The compelling conditions for British advances in tropical Africa were first called into being, not by the German victory of 1871, nor by Leopold's interest in the Congo, nor by the petty rivalry of missionaries and merchants, nor by a rising imperialist spirit, nor even by the French occupation of Tunis in 1881—but by the collapse of the Khedivial *régime* in Egypt.

From start to finish the partition of tropical Africa was driven by the persistent crisis in Egypt. When the British entered Egypt on their own, the Scramble began; and as long as they stayed in Cairo, it continued until there was no more of Africa left to divide. Since chance and miscalculation had much to do with the way that Britain went into Egypt, it was to some extent an accident that the partition took place when it did. But once it had begun, Britain's over-riding purpose in Africa was security in Egypt, the Mediterranean and the Orient....

Both the crisis of expansion and the official mind which attempted to control them had their origins in an historical process which had begun to unfold long before the partition of Africa began. That movement was not the manifestation of some revolutionary urge to empire. Its deeper causes do not lie in the last two decades of the century. The British advance at least, was not an isolated African episode. It was the climax of a longer process of growth and decay in Africa. The new African empire was improvised by the official mind, as events made nonsense of its old historiography and hustled government into strange deviations from old lines of policy. In the widest sense, it was an offshoot of the total processes of British expansion throughout the world and throughout the century....

...The partition of tropical Africa might seem impressive on the wall maps of the Foreign Office. Yet it was at the time an empty and theoretical expansion. That British governments before 1900 did very little to pacify, administer and develop their spheres of influence and protectorates, shows once again the weakness of any commercial and imperial motives for claiming them. The partition did not accompany, it preceded the invasion of tropical Africa by the trader, the planter and the official. It was the prelude to European occupation; it was not that occupation itself. The sequence illuminates the true nature of the British movement into tropical Africa. So far from commercial expansion requiring the extension of territorial claims, it was the extension of claims which in time required commercial expansion....

Suggested Additional Readings

The literature of imperialism, imperial expansion, and empire is vast. Much of it is polemical, propaganda designed to demonstrate that one nation's imperial policies were beneficial to the world and its subject peoples while another nation's imperial policies led to war and a degraded colonial proletariat. But there is a considerable body of both scholarly and popular writing on problems related to imperialism, and the size and quality of this body is increasing rapidly. An expanded interest in the "political collapse of Europe," as the historian Hajo Holborn has phrased it, as evidenced overseas; the sudden rise of new African and Asian nationalisms, with an accompanying interest in the colonial history of the new nations; and a major expansion of area-studies programs, particularly in the United States, with emphasis on African, South Asian, and Southeast Asian studies—areas intimately associated with imperialism—all have led to the beginnings of a new assessment of national expansion, a new assessment that will require hundreds of case studies, articles, and monographs before the major works of synthesis so badly needed can be written. In short, there is much activity; there are many articles and intensive studies; and as yet there is no really sound, analytical, broadly-based survey of, in particular, British imperialism. But there are many good books which one may read in preparation for the broader work of sythesis.

Nor is there any bibliographical reference work which brings together all of the titles relating to imperialism. To prepare such a reference would require much effort and time, for the number of titles now runs into the thousands. An early, somewhat limited, bibliography, reasonably comprehensive to the date of its publication, is Lowell J. Ragatz, *The Literature of European Imperialism, 1815–1939: A Bibliography* (Washington, 1944). Also of value, although somewhat out-of-date, is Wesley Frank Craven, "Historical Study of the British Empire," *The Journal of Modern History,* VI (March 1934), 40–69. Ragatz raises some interesting questions in "Must We Rewrite the History of Imperialism?" *Historical Studies: Australia and New Zealand,* VI (November 1953), 90–98. A more recent assessment, by one of the leading American scholars in the field, is Philip D. Curtin, "The British Empire and Commonwealth in Recent Historiography," *The American Historical Review,* LXV (October 1959), 72–91. Harrison M. Wright has prepared a book of readings similar to the present one under the title *The "New Imperialism": Analysis of Late Nineteenth-Century Expansion* (Boston, 1961), which contains a good bibliography.

Four booklets of historiographical and bibliographical interest also will prove of use to the student: Charles F. Mullett, *The British Empire-Commonwealth: Its Themes and Character. A Plural Society in Evolution* (Washington, 1961); Robin W. Winks, *Recent Trends and New Literature in Canadian History* (Washington, 1959); and Robert I. Crane, *The History of India: Its Study and Interpretation* (Washington, 1958), all publications of the American Historical Association's Service Center for Teachers of History; and W. P. Morrell, *British Overseas Expansion and the History of the Commonwealth: A Select Bibliography* (London, 1961). In

1964 Duke University Press will publish a book of historiographical reappraisals of British Empire-Commonwealth history containing twenty essays, edited by the compiler of the present booklet. Finally, James G. Allen, *The British Empire and Commonwealth: A Syllabus and Guide to Reading* (3d ed.; Boulder, Colo., 1953), also is quite helpful.

There are few general works on imperialism. Standard accounts of European expansion include Parker T. Moon, *Imperialism and World Politics* (New York, 1926); Mary E. Townsend and Cyrus H. Peake, *European Colonial Expansion since 1871* (Chicago, 1941); and to some extent A.P. Newton, *A Hundred Years of the British Empire* (London, 1940). Basic texts of the British Empire-Commonwealth includes volumes by A.L. Burt, Paul Knaplund, C.E. Carrington, W.R. Brock, and R.G. Trotter. Halford L. Hoskins, *European Imperialism in Africa* (New York, 1930), while old is still a convenient summary. For the recent period Stewart C. Easton, *Twilight of European Colonialism* (New York, 1960) is sound. An interesting general study of the theories of imperialism is E. M. Winslow, *The Pattern of Imperialism: A Study in the Theories of Power* (New York, 1948).

Most general studies, and notably the volumes by Moon, Townsend and Peake, and Winslow, have tended to accept as proved the primacy of economic motives for imperialism. The literature on the various economic theories of empire is considerable, but there are a number of convenient guides and discussions of the various points of view. Most useful are Daniel H. Kruger, "Hobson, Lenin, and Schumpeter on Imperialism," *Journal of the History of Ideas,* XVI (April 1955), 252–259, which summarizes well but adds little that is original; two articles by Horace B. Davis written from a Marxist point of view: "Conservative Writers on Imperialism," *Science and Society,* XVIII (Fall 1954), 310–325, and "Imperialism and Labor: An Analysis of Marxian Views," *ibid.,* XXVI (Winter 1962), 26–45, which concludes that the laboring man actually prospered during the major wave of imperial expansion; Brynjolf J. Hovde, "Socialistic Theories of Imperialism Prior to the Great War," *The Journal of Political Economy,* XXXVI (October 1928), 569–591; and Leonard Woolf, *Economic Imperialism* (London, 1921). Most recently John Strachey has revived the Marxist interpretation in *The End of Empire* (London, 1959).

Among those who are critical of the economic interpretation are D. K. Fieldhouse and Mark Blaug, quoted in the present booklet; Raymond Aron, "The Leninist Myth of Imperialism," *Partisan Review,* XVIII (December 1951), 646–662; several of the authors in Robert Strausz-Hupé and Harry W. Hazard, eds., *The Idea of Colonialism* (New York, 1958); Hans J. Morgenthau, *Politics Among Nations: The Struggle for Power and Peace* (3d ed.; New York, 1960); Reinhold Niebuhr, *The Structure of Nations and Empires* (New York, 1959); Lionel Robbins, *The Economic Causes of War* (London, 1939); and Richard Koebner, "The Concept of Economic Imperialism," *Economic History Review,* 2d ser., II (1949), 1–29. Also of interest in this regard are Richard Pares, "The Economic Factors in the History of the Empire," *ibid.,* VII (May 1937), 119–144; and C. E. Carrington, *An Exposition of Empire* (Cambridge, 1947).

There still can be no answer to the question, Did colonies pay? for the question means many different things. In *A Place in the Sun* (New York, 1936), Grover Clark says the answer must be, "emphatically . . . No." Yet A. K. Cairncross, *Home and Foreign Investment 1870–1913* (Cambridge, 1953), concludes that after a fashion they did. The reader also should refer to those titles cited in the Fieldhouse selection, above, and to S. B. Saul, *Studies in British Overseas Trade 1870–1914* (Liverpool, 1960).

Nor can there be any resolution to the problem of whether colonies were ultimately beneficial to the subjected peoples. R. Palme Dutt, a leader of the Communist movement in England, presents the negative view in *The Crisis of Britain and the British Empire* (rev. ed.; London, 1957). Margery Perham, in *The Colonial Reckoning* (New York, 1962), provides a more positive balance sheet.

There are many volumes on special themes of British imperialism. Within its limits C. A. Bodelson, *Studies in Mid-Victorian Imperialism* (Copenhagen, 1934), still is worth reading. On the missionary influence, Harrison Wright, *New Zealand, 1769–1840: Early Years of Western Contact* (Cambridge, Mass., 1959), and Roland Oliver, *The Missionary Factor in East Africa* (London, 1952), are particularly good. On the broader background Kenneth Scott Latourette, *Christianity in a Revolutionary Age*, vol. III: *The Nineteenth Century Outside Europe* (New York, 1961), is quite useful. On the new romantic literature of the time biographies of H. Rider Haggard and Rudyard Kipling are available, and others of their school are examined with wit and insight in Richard Usborne, *Clubland Heroes* (London, 1953). Susanne Howe, *Novels of Empire* (New York, 1949), is straightforward but useful, while George D. Bearce, *British Attitudes toward India, 1784–1858* (New York, 1961), is particularly good. Excellent case studies of the type so badly needed are C. D. Cowan, *Nineteenth-Century Malaya: The Origins of British Political Control* (London, 1961), which shows British expansion in Southeast Asia to have stemmed from essentially noneconomic factors; and David S. Landes, *Bankers and Pashas: International Finance and Economic Imperialism in Egypt* (Cambridge, Mass., 1958), which is largely concerned with the French. Donald G. Creighton, "The Victorians and the Empire," *The Canadian Historical Review,* XIX (March 1938), 138–153, is reprinted in Robert L. Schuyler and Herman Ausubel, eds., *The Making of English History* (New York, 1952).

Bernard Semmel, *Imperialism and Social Reform* (Cambridge, Mass., 1960) is important; so too is vol. XXI (December 1961) of *The Journal of Economic History,* the entire issue being devoted to colonialism. The role of "the man on the spot," the local administrator, is examined by John S. Galbraith in "The 'Turbulent Frontier' as a Factor in British Expansion," *Comparative Studies in Society and History,* II (January 1960), 150–168. The relationship of imperialism to the outbreak of World War I has received close study, and every book on the causes of the war would be pertinent here, but the reader should begin with William L. Langer, *The Diplomacy of Imperialism,* 2 vols. (New York, 1935), and his *European Alliances and Alignments, 1871–1890* (New York, 1931). A recent collection of readings which is of both synthetic and bibliographical use is Louis L. Snyder, ed., *The Imperialism Reader* (Princeton, 1962).